small business
websites that work

small business websites that work

get online to grow your company

Sean McManus

www.sbwtw.com

Prentice Hall

An imprint of **Pearson Education**

London · New York · San Francisco · Toronto · Sydney
Tokyo · Singapore · Hong Kong · Cape Town · Madrid
Paris · Milan · Munich · Amsterdam

PEARSON EDUCATION LIMITED

Head Office
Edinburgh Gate
Harlow CM20 2JE
Tel: +44 (0)1279 623623
Fax: +44 (0)1279 431059

London Office:
128 Long Acre, London WC2E 9AN
Tel: +44 (0)20 7447 2000
Fax: +44 (0)20 7240 5771
Website:www.business-minds.com

First published in Great Britain in 2001

ISBN 0 273 65486 1

British Library Cataloguing in Publication Data
A CIP catalogue record for this book can be obtained from the British Library.

10 9 8 7 6 5 4 3 2 1

Designed by Sue Lamble
Typeset by Pantek Arts Ltd, Maidstone, Kent
Printed and bound in Great Britain by Bell & Bain Ltd, Glasgow

The Publishers' policy is to use paper manufactured from sustainable forests.

About the author

Sean McManus is a consultant and journalist. He studied International Business at Aston University and has been building websites and consulting small businesses on their online strategy for three years.

Among other things, his articles have explored how to make websites usable by the blind, how perfumiers hope to send smells over the Internet, and how to personalize your site with a cartoon avatar. His articles have appeared in magazines including *Business 2.0*, *Internet Works*, *Internet Magazine*, *Personal Computer World*, *Customer Loyalty Today* and *Marketing Week*.

He is the co-author with Alison Alsbury of *Quick Answers to Key Web Marketing Questions*.

In his spare time, Sean looks after his personal site at www.sean.co.uk.

Contents

Acknowledgements

I'd like to thank everyone who has offered encouragement during this project, particularly Amelia Lakin at Pearson for her enthusiasm and guidance. Thanks also to Rachael Stock at Pearson for picking up on the original proposal, and the Society of Authors for advice. Thanks to Linda Dhondy and Vivienne Church, who project-managed and copy-edited this book respectively.

Nik Scott's excellent 'Cran and Lerma' cartoons appear in this book, appropriately enough, as a result of his own successful website promotion and our subsequent e-mail cooperation. Many thanks to him. More of his cartoons can be found at www.nikscott.com.

I'd like to thank everyone who responded promptly to screenshot and research requests and allowed their insights to appear in this book. Special thanks for time given generously must go to Nancy A. Taffera-Santos and Jeff Seacrist at Webtrends, Joseph Householder and Dean Harvey of Vinson & Elkins L.L.P., Steve Almond of Barclays Merchant Services, and Nazir Jessa of Savastore.

I would also like to thank the many businesses, big and small, that have allowed their screenshots to appear in this book to illustrate key ideas that you can use in growing your own company. In order of appearance these are: Google Inc; Microsoft Corporation; Netscape Communications; Amazon.com Inc; Art Wolfe; Everything2; John Hartnup; Rowan Lipkovits; University of California, Berkeley; Iprint.com Inc; Aurora Luggage; Midas Entertainment; eSynch/Kiss Software Corp; Funplanet AB; Internet Florist Association; Americanese Inc; Hector Duran; Booktailor Ltd; Bustamove Inc; Moreover; iPIX; Iglu.com; Dan McDonald; Netmechanic Inc; Communication Enabling Technologies; Rob Rosenberger; Humanclick; Microsoft Corporation; Webtrends.

Most of the screenshots in this book feature the Internet Explorer browser and are reprinted by permission from Microsoft Corporation.

Thanks to Derek Williams for introducing me to some of the business ideas over the last few years that have shaped my thinking and to Peter Sayer for encouragement reading draft chapters. Special thanks to Karen Holland for finding the time and having the patience to read the draft book and offer helpful feedback.

Introduction

Your business is at stake if you delegate responsibility for
more than your website designers can handle

Why you should read this book

Who should read this book

The book's website

How this book is organized

How to use this book

Why you should read this book

Will a website designer understand your business and your customers as intimately as you do? Even the best designers probably have no background in marketing, no previous contact with your target audience, and little experience in setting a corporate website strategy. Your business is at stake if you delegate responsibility for more than they can handle.

That's why it is important that you learn enough about how the Internet works, and how your business will benefit from having a website, to be able to manage the design team. If your website designers are to support your company – and not the other way around – you need to be independent of them. They have a vested interest in selling you website services, so it's vital that you can assess their proposals from the perspective of what the business needs.

This book will walk you through the decisions you need to make in commissioning a website for your organization and managing the team responsible. It will show you how to create and promote a successful website. You could just put your existing brochure online, but it's easy to build a site that will generate a better response from the marketplace and will enable you to engage the Internet community more fully. This book shows how.

Who should read this book

This book is ideal for:

- managers and sole traders who need to understand the opportunities their website offers and how to exploit them fully;

- marketing managers who want to see how the web can help improve profitability, improve customer relationships, and cut the cost of customer acquisition;

- website designers who want to learn how they can provide business solutions and not just website designs.

Your company might be looking to set up its first website, or might be dissatisfied with the results from the existing site. In either case, the book delivers ideas for how you can use the technology to grow your company.

The book's website

This book has its own regularly updated website to guide you to online case studies, to further reading and to tools that will help you to manage your site. The website makes it possible to provide links to resources which might not last the shelf life of a book and to new websites as they become available. The website includes all the links from the book, but also many that aren't in the book.

At the website you can also join the mailing list for news on book and website updates.

To visit the website for *Small Business Websites That Work*, go to www.sbwtw.com

How this book is organized

Getting to know the Internet

How can you judge your website if it's the only one you've seen? This chapter tells you why the Internet matters to business, and provides a tour of websites that showcase the web's potential.

Planning your website and creating the content

If you don't know what your website will do for your business, it will only be profitable by accident. This chapter starts by asking why you might want to have a website, and goes on to discuss 11 ways your website can improve your business. The chapter also explains how you can use website content to attract and keep customers, and includes case studies of small businesses that are thinking beyond putting their brochure online. There is also guidance on planning your content and writing for the web.

Resourcing your website design

Once you know why you're creating a website and what it will contain, it's time to think about who will design it. This chapter compares your options: bringing someone in-house, outsourcing the work, or doing it yourself. There's a pay-off between control and cost, but as this chapter shows, what might seem like the cheapest option can turn out to be the most expensive.

Naming and hosting your website

Your existing customers will find your site by typing in its domain name, so it needs to be memorable. This chapter guides you in choosing a good name and will tell you what to look out for when deciding where the site will be hosted. With good names being registered all the time, you must stake your territory as soon as you're confident you've found the right name.

What makes a good website?

Now your design team is ready to develop the site, you need to look more closely at what makes a good design. This chapter explains the limitations your designers have to work with, and what they should be doing to get around them. It highlights often-seen design crimes and explains the minimum technical background you need to make sure that the site is as fast and easy to use as possible.

Making money through advertising and affiliate programmes

Everywhere you go online you see promotions offering you '$$$' for linking to a website. Can you really make money like this? This chapter points out the pitfalls and tells you how to make a success of affiliate programmes.

Selling from your website

For many businesses, the web gives them a chance to engage in distance-selling for the first time. This chapter discusses how you can encourage customers to buy from your website, how you can accept credit cards, and what security you'll need.

Offering great customer service online

You must be able to respond to enquiries promptly. It takes seconds to write an e-mail, so customers expect a fast reply. This chapter explains how to introduce customer service by e-mail into your business and warns of the risks of viruses and other e-mail nuisances.

Promoting your website

For most successful sites, this is where the real hard work begins. It won't be enough to just register with search engines if you want to make the most of your opportunities online. This chapter explains all the different ways you can promote your website, both online and off-line, including tips on writing press releases, an insight into how search engines rank websites, and the importance of links. As these ideas show, effective promotion doesn't cost much but does need time and commitment.

Keeping your website legal and ethical

How can national laws legislate websites that are available everywhere? This chapter discusses how you can limit your risk using a clear privacy policy and terms and conditions of use for your website. Although test cases are few and far between, leaving lawyers uncertain how the law will be applied to the web, it's as much a case of keeping the site ethical as it is of second-guessing how judges will think.

Measuring your website's success

You can only manage what you measure, but that doesn't have to be just the traffic running through your site. This chapter explains how you can tell whether your site is meeting its business objectives or not. It's the last chapter in the book, but it's also the start of the next wave of site design and promotion. Accurate information on how your website is performing will stop you repeating mistakes or false assumptions as your website grows.

Glossary

The glossary explains terms that are used throughout the book.

How to use this book

Each chapter can be read independently. Chapters are cross-referenced where appropriate to help you find what you need throughout the book. Each chapter starts with an 'at a glance' menu of what's coming up and ends with a summary.

'Technology tips' lists are used to clearly explain what you (or someone in your company) must know about website design to manage the designers effectively. Checklists are used to give you a quick guide to what's important.

Case studies (of real companies) and examples (of imaginary companies) are used throughout the book to put the ideas in context. Hopefully these websites will still be available when you come to visit them, but the important lessons are included in the book, together with screenshots where appropriate. A company's inclusion in this book shouldn't be taken as an endorsement that everything the site is doing is necessarily right, but should still give you sparkling ideas you can use in your own business.

You're encouraged to visit the book's official website at www.sbwtw.com for links and additional information to go with each chapter. The site includes many links to further reading and online tools that are not in the book.

Getting to know the Internet

You can't imagine how your visitors will want to use your site if you haven't experienced the best, and the worst, of other websites

Introduction

How can you tell how good your website is if it's the only one you've seen? How can you assess the opportunities if you don't know what the competition is doing? You can't imagine how your visitors will want to use your site if you haven't experienced the best, and the worst, of other websites.

This chapter will give you a quick tour of the Internet. It will arm you with the background knowledge you need before you can start thinking seriously about how your site will grow your business.

What is the Internet?

Like most technology, the Internet grew from military research. In the late Sixties work began on a communications network that would survive a nuclear attack. Messages were sent out over the network with instructions to say where they were coming from and who they were going to, and travelled through the network using any surviving paths to reach their destination. The network was used mainly by academics throughout the Seventies and Eighties and grew steadily, but in the early Nineties the world wide web was created.

The web provided a standardized way to present information online, making the Internet easier to use. Pages could be linked to each other, so that instead of reading documents like a book, you could leap between any pages according to which ideas you wanted to pursue. Around the same time, businesses started to take an interest.

Now the world wide web is available to most people in industrialized countries through work, internet cafes, public libraries and home computers. For the cost of a local phone call, or in many cases a toll-free number, users can connect to the Internet and view pages stored on servers all over the world.

Nine important effects of the Internet on business

The internet has nine important effects on how small businesses market themselves.

1 All businesses, whatever their industry, are competing for the customer's time on the Internet. In the same way that TV adverts compete with programmes on the other channel, your website competes with entertainment and information sites by industry leaders. If your customers are bored, they'll go somewhere more interesting. You need to offer customers something of value to them to get them to visit your website and come back. That doesn't mean it has to be expensive to you: good information can be priceless to readers but cheap to research and write. Ordering without queuing in a shop can be enticing enough. See Chapter 2 for ideas on how your site can help your customers and your business.

2 Your website is a product of the company, albeit one you give away. It needs an investment in designing it, producing it and promoting it like any other product or service. Small businesses that have limited their marketing to an advert in the phone book might have to be more creative and become small-scale publishers to make the most of their opportunities online. Some of the marketing effort needs to shift away from trying to sell things or push the company and move towards evangelizing the benefits of visiting the website if it is to achieve its potential. See Chapter 9 for advice on promoting your website.

3 Communications with customers are more timely. You can update online catalogues in minutes at any hour of the day or night without incurring the reprint and postage costs associated with paper copies. Using e-mail, you can afford to make greater customer contact part of your service and can tell customers as soon as you learn something they might be interested in.

4 You need customers' participation in your promotions. Customers must choose to visit your website, whether that is by copying your address off a carrier bag, clicking on a link on another site or choosing your site before others listed in a search engine. If customers don't want to read your e-mails, they won't even open them. On the Internet you can't easily achieve the same passive awareness of a business that a storefront, newspaper advert or a local radio jingle can.

5 Shops and other walk-in businesses need to evolve to compete with websites that can offer similar services at a lower cost or that choose to operate at a loss to secure market share. Walk-in businesses must show customers the strength of personal service and focus on the experience of making a visit.

6 The Internet enables more sophisticated relationships with customers. Websites can automatically harvest information on visitors, or can use sophisticated programming to recommend products based on customers' preferences or previous purchases. Customers will reveal marketing information to you that you could never glean from a phone call or shop visit if you give them something of value in return.

7 Customers can often compare prices at a click, so you must concentrate on differentiating your business on quality and not price. Otherwise you will be forced to match the silliest 'yard sale' prices that other websites are offering. And given that anyone could sell their second-hand goods online, you can't be sure that those prices will exceed even the lowest costs businesses incur.

8 On the Internet, markets are split by sector and not by region. Independent hi-fi shops are sustained by the fact that customers won't travel to the next city to buy a radio they can buy locally. But if those customers buy online, it doesn't matter where the goods are coming from and local shops must compete with the best sites in the world.

9 Customers are forced to judge businesses by their online competence. When shopping online, there is no other demonstration of quality. Customers are often expected to give their credit card details to a company they know only from its website. Businesses must win and confirm the customer's trust in them with everything they do.

The internet is changing not only how companies deal with customers but also how they work with their team members and supply chain too. You don't necessarily need to have people cluttering up your office as long as they can all access the same files. Projects can now be managed over the Internet so that wherever team members may be, they can plug into the file archive through a simple but secure website. You might be able to create a purchasing system for your raw materials that enables you to link your inventory management software automatically to ordering systems. Internal e-mail can make it much easier for you to keep in touch with your company and helps to standardize communications with the outside world.

These benefits affect how your company uses the Internet and spin-off technologies internally. This book won't deal with these, focusing instead on your own public corner of the Internet: your website. But be aware of how the Internet might help you integrate with partner companies.

CASE STUDY

Savastore savings

Savastore (www.savastore.com) set up its website in 1997 (when it was called watford.co.uk) and has been able to cut its inventory by 55 per cent as a result. The company previously warehoused more than 6,000 lines of computer products and sold them by mail order and in its shops. But using the website, and integrating more closely with suppliers, has enabled the company to cut its inventory.

It works like this. Customers order from the website and pay by credit card. The credit card is checked automatically for authorization and the customer's name and address are cross-referenced against a database of UK addresses. Customers can be asked to try again, or the order can be directed for personal intervention by staff. This has cut fraudulent transactions to 0.01 per cent.

The order is then fed automatically to the company's resource planning system, which scans suppliers' warehouses for availability and places an order. If more than one supplier can fulfil the order, it goes to the cheapest. Savastore has renegotiated contracts with suppliers so that it now buys goods at cost price plus a fixed markup instead of having different margins across different products.

The supplier electronically informs Savastore when the order is dispatched with the courier information and Savastore passes this on to the customer via e-mail. Using the tracking code in the e-mail, the customer can get an estimated delivery time from the courier's website. Only once the order has been signed for is the credit card debited.

The savings include:

- reduced breakage and shrinkage by single handling of the goods;
- reduced traffic in Savastore's warehouse, cutting staffing and storage costs;
- in excess of £120,000 (around US$180,000) because more than 100,000 invoices are sent by e-mail instead of by post each year;
- datasheets on the website which replace the need to send printed information.

Should the customer e-mail a complaint, it is distributed to someone in the customer service department. If it goes unanswered after ten minutes, it escalates to the manager. Within two hours, unanswered complaints escalate to the company directors.

By using the Internet to integrate its company with suppliers, Savastore is able to take responsibility for the customers' satisfaction with the service and the products without having to carry the stock.

'A strategy like this must come from the senior management and not from the technical people to achieve best results,' says Nazir Jessa the MD.

How people access the Internet

Most people will use a computer like a PC or a Macintosh and will run software such as Netscape Navigator or Microsoft Internet Explorer that shows them web pages and lets them interact with them.

Internet service providers (ISPs) are the companies that provide a connection to the Internet. The computer connects to the ISP over a phone line, or by cable or another network, and this is used to send page requests and pages back and forth.

Some people will access the Internet on mobile devices, such as phones. Others might use speech browsers, games consoles or WebTV.

This book includes ideas that are applicable to all these technologies, but assumes most people will be using computers.

Here's how websites work when using Netscape Navigator or Internet Explorer.

- You move your pointer around the screen with the mouse.
- You can go straight to a web page by entering its address (also known as its URL) in the location bar just above where the web page starts.
- Links are usually underlined in text, but any text or graphic could be a link. If your pointer turns into a hand when you move the mouse over something, it's a link.
- When you click on a link, you're taken to another page. Sometimes it will open a new window for that page. Spending time visiting websites and following the links between them is known as surfing the web.
- You have buttons at the top of the screen to go back, to stop a page loading or to reload or refresh the page.
- You can store a link to pages you like in your favourites or bookmarks folder. This is called bookmarking the page. Next time you want to visit them, you just choose them from the bookmarks and the page will be downloaded over the Internet.
- When the icon in the top right of the screen is moving, it means the page is loading.
- You can print web pages by going to the File menu and selecting print.

Part of the Internet's appeal is that you can learn how to use it in minutes and become an expert at reading web pages in about an hour. If you're not familiar with the Internet already, this could be the best hour you ever invest in your personal development and will open a new world of information and entertainment to you.

Fourteen websites you must see

The more websites you visit, the more ideas you'll pick up. You'll notice what frustrates visitors and what works well. And you'll be in a stronger position to steer your own business website. You'll know what's realistic, what's ideal, and what you want to avoid at all costs.

Here's a whirlwind tour of some sites you should see.

A search engine: Google.com

There are lots of search engines, and they all differ slightly. Google (www.google.com) prides itself on being the fastest. Search engines help you to find web pages. You enter keywords that describe what you're looking for and are given pages of results with short descriptions of the sites and links to them. Don't be daunted: it's extremely rare to get only a few results and it's often easier to come up with better search keywords than it is to plough through thousands of results. One feature of Google is the 'I'm feeling lucky' button, which will take you straight to the site that ranks top in the list. Other search engines include www.hotbot.com, www.lycos.com and www.altavista.com.

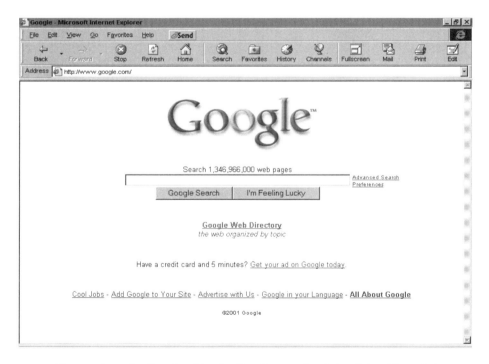

The search engine Google prides itself on the speed and simplicity of its website

Screenshot courtesy of Google Inc.
Screenshot of Internet Explorer browser reprinted by permission of Microsoft Corporation

A search directory: The Open Directory Project

Search engines compile their databases automatically. Search directories are edited by people who review sites and file them in the relevant categories. That way, surfers just need to find the right category to discover lots of similar sites together. Categories are arranged hierarchically, so that music comes under arts, for example, and opera is placed below music. The Open Directory website is at www.dmoz.org. Volunteers edit this directory and anyone is free to use it, or any portion of it, on their own website free of charge. As well as showing how directories work, it's a good illustration of how the Internet community can work together. The pioneering directory was Yahoo (www.yahoo.com).

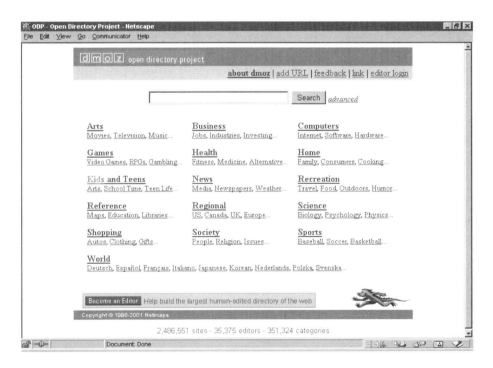

The Open Directory at www.dmoz.org **is a catalogue that you can use to find sites to visit and can adapt for publication on your own website.**

Image courtesy of Netscape Communications

9

Your competitors' websites: you'll have to find them first

You can use search engines and directories to find your competitors' websites. Have a look so you can see how to differentiate yourself and what ideas are widely used on websites in your industry. It's also a good time to ferret out some amateur home pages and surf around sites that cover your interests. Find a directory category you like, and visit several of the sites there.

An e-commerce site: Amazon.com

Amazon (www.amazon.com) set the standard for selling consumer goods online by making online shopping more convenient and supporting it with strong customer service. The site began by selling books and now offers products as diverse as cameras and garden furniture. When you visit Amazon, look out for the following features:

- shopping cart: when you choose a product you're taken to a screen called the shopping cart. You can keep putting products here until you're ready to finish shopping and buy everything;

- product reviews: customers are encouraged to tell others what they thought about a product, whether it's good or bad;

- articles: the site features interviews with authors and musicians to promote their products, and tutorials for the photography section. You can visit the site for information as well as shopping;

- recommendations: if you buy something at Amazon or set up an account at the site, the site will greet you by name and tell you about products it thinks you'll like based on what you've bought before;

- search box on every page: you can find books by title or author and can find other products by keywords;

- associates programme: Amazon was a pioneer in affiliate programmes where websites are paid a commission for referring shoppers to Amazon;

- wish lists: come Christmas time or birthdays, you can set up a list of presents you'd like at Amazon and your family and friends can buy them directly at the site.

Amazon's photography store includes tutorials and tips from expert photographers

A news website: BBC.co.uk

The Internet is changing the pace of news. When news no longer has to wait for a scheduled bulletin on the radio, or go through the production process of a printed publication, it becomes nearly instant. The site of the UK's public service broadcaster the BBC (www.bbc.co.uk) is one of the leading news websites. Suddenly anything published online with last week's date looks very old indeed.

A music website: MP3.com

MP3 is a file format used for downloading songs from the Internet and storing them to play back later. This website gives bands a showcase to give away their MP3s and sell their CDs which are manufactured on demand. While some record labels have been concerned about listeners pirating music over the Internet, MP3.com embodies the freedom that this technology gives new musicians to reach a global audience. The musicians' problem changes from how to access the distribution channels (record labels, record shops, radio stations) to how to convince listeners flooded with free music to download theirs, keep it and buy the next album.

A web-based e-mail website: Hotmail.com

E-mail enables people to exchange messages with each other directly. They're sent out over the Internet and sit in the recipient's e-mail box until that person uses software to collect them. Hotmail (www.hotmail.com) is a web-based e-mail service, which means that people don't need to have any dedicated e-mail software to collect their e-mail. They can just use this specially designed website in a normal web browser and click on links and use on-screen forms to collect messages or write new messages. Hotmail offers free e-mail accounts to anyone who wants them.

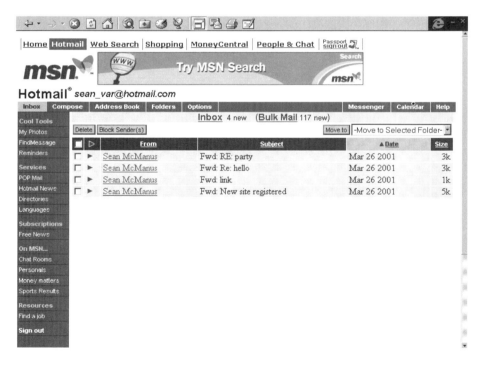

Hotmail provides free e-mail accounts that are accessed through a web browser

Screenshot reprinted by permission from Microsoft Corporation

A community website: Everything2.com

Websites often exist to give their visitors a voice. The website sets the parameters for discussion and visitors then exchange views on the site. Everything2 (www.everything2.com) is like an encyclopaedia written with an anarchic sense of humour, and with everyone able to contribute. Visitors can create nodes of information and link them to other nodes of information, so that readers can keep clicking through diverse ideas until they want to add a thought of their own. The quality of the contributions varies, but there are some imaginative articles here that would not otherwise have been published.

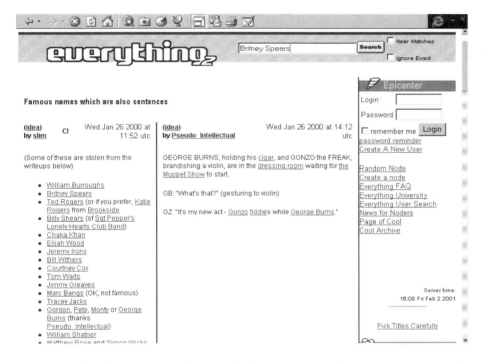

Everything2 has a community of contributors who are creating a virtual encyclopaedia with a twist

Screenshot courtesy of Everything Development. Website structure by Nate Oostendorp. Idea attributed to Slim by and courtesy of John Hartnup. Idea attributed to Pseudo Intellectual by and courtesy of Rowan Lipkovits

A Flash animation website: Sesamestreet.com

Most of this book argues against using animation on websites because it's distracting and it gets in the way of your goals to communicate quickly with customers. But this is a great example of what can be achieved when the audience will be influenced by good presentation and will be prepared to wait. Here, the animation is an important part of the website's appeal to its audience of children. You'll need the Flash animation plug-in to use it (more about plug-ins in Chapter 5).

Cooperating online: Seti@home

Seti@home (short for Search for Extraterrestrial Intelligence at Home) is a project that is scanning radio telescope signals for messages from aliens. Volunteers download a program from the website and a file of

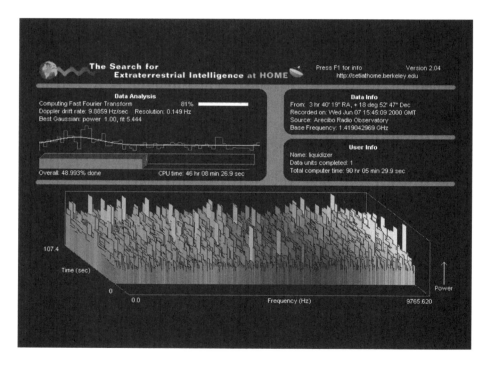

The Seti@home software processes radio telescope data looking for intelligent alien signals. Work units are exchanged over the Internet and users have combined to make the world's largest supercomputer

Screenshot courtesy of Seti@home, University of California, Berkeley

telescope data. When the volunteer's computer is not in use, the screensaver crunches through the data looking for signals that might suggest intelligent life out there. The results are sent back to the project's headquarters over the Internet, and the volunteer downloads another chunk of data to process. Previously there was too much data from the telescope each night to analyze, but now with the combined donations of small chunks of processing time, Seti@home has created the largest supercomputer in the world. Companies have since been set up to farm out processing jobs over similar networks commercially. The website is really only a small part of this project, but Seti@home is a good demonstration of what you can do if you mobilize the Internet community for the global good. Visit www.setiathome.ssl.berkeley.edu to take part.

An auctions site: Ebay.com

Ebay (www.ebay.com) is like a worldwide yard sale. Anyone can advertise their goods on the website and anyone can bid to buy them. At the end of the auction period, the highest bidder wins. When visiting the site, look out for:

- The ability to search auctions by keyword.

- automated bidding: you can set a limit on how much you're prepared to pay and Ebay will automatically increase your bid in steps if someone outbids you until you've hit your maximum;

- Buyer and seller ratings: after a transaction has been completed, buyers and sellers can rate each other on the site so that future traders know how trustworthy they are. This makes the community self-policing.

A routing website: Mapquest.com

Visitors to Mapquest (www.mapquest.com) can enter the start and end points of their journey and receive turn-by-turn driving instructions on how to get there. It's an example of how the Internet is releasing data from physical constraints. Increasingly people expect information to be available in the form they need it, and the web can help to make that possible.

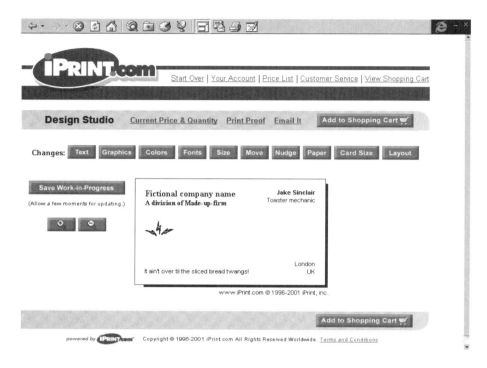

Iprint.com enables customers to use a web browser to design their own business cards which are then printed and delivered by post

Screenshot courtesy of Iprint.com Inc

A mass customization website: Iprint.com

Mass production in the past meant that all the products were the same. But Iprint (www.iprint.com) is using the Internet to gather information about products which is then fed electronically to the machinery that makes them. Customers can design their own business cards by clicking on links and buttons and entering information in online forms. Other products available include mousemats, magnetic signs, address labels and keychains.

A portal: MSN

A portal is a site that's designed as a gateway to the Internet. It typically combines news, a free e-mail account, shopping and search engines and often includes articles written just for that portal's visitors. MSN (www.msn.com) is Microsoft's portal and it has different regional versions

MSN offers feature articles, news and special offers as well as e-mail and shopping

Screenshot reprinted by permission from Microsoft Corporation

depending on which country you're accessing it from. Most people will have a portal set as their browser's default start page when they install it.

This isn't an exhaustive portrait of what the Internet can do, but there's one thing all websites have in common. They're all about exchanging information. It might be information on where to find websites you need, or somebody's views on popular culture. It might be the to and fro of bidding in an auction or the advertising of products. Or it might be the exchange of computer files containing song recordings or scientific data.

Think about what information is important in your industry and what you might be able to do commercially now the technology exists to distribute it quickly all over the world, through the day and night.

Summary

You need to be familiar with the Internet so that you can judge how your own site measures up. Visiting other sites is also the best way to come up with new ideas for your site.

The Internet is changing how small businesses market themselves and changing the nature of competition. Companies must focus on differentiating themselves on quality and must encourage their customers to interact with them outside of normal business.

It only takes an hour to teach yourself to read web pages and surf the web, and if you're not already using the Internet this could be the best small investment you make in your career. The suggested sites give a good insight into some of what the Internet is capable of, and what many of your visitors will already have seen when they arrive at your website.

Planning your website and creating the content

Nobody knows your business better than you do.If you don't tell your website designers how your website will improve your business, it will only be profitable by accident

Introduction

With the promise of a global marketplace aching for your products, it's easy to be seduced on to the Internet. The cost of setting up a website can seem small compared to the potential benefits.

But stop and think. Why does your company need a website? The web is groaning under the weight of pages hastily launched that do nothing to improve their companies' businesses. Many of them cost a lot of time and money to create and maintain.

You must start by working out how a website can help meet your company's goals. This is not something you can leave to the last minute – it must be at the heart of the content, the design brief, the technology and the business processes.

You can outsource the development of your website (more about that in Chapter 3), but you must take responsibility for its strategy at a senior level within your company. Nobody knows your business better than you do, least of all your web design company. They won't have researched your market, so if you don't tell them how your website is supposed to improve your business, it will only be profitable by accident.

Some bad reasons to have a website

Internet myth you must have a website

Unless it's going to help your business, why bother? You wouldn't print a batch of brochures for the fun of it or exhibit at a show without knowing who's visiting. Be sure of how your website will help your organization.

Sometimes companies consider going online because 'it's about time' they did, or because there's someone on the team who wants to make it their pet project.

Companies often feel pressured by their competitors having a website. But your rivals could be investing a lot of money and suffering huge losses. It could strengthen your competitive position not to incur that cost. The money might be better allocated to advertising or improved customer service.

If you feel you need to have an Internet presence, consider the other reasons for having a website and the potential benefits first. Any site designed purely out of a feeling that there must be one is unlikely to lift profits much.

Eleven ways your website can help your business

Here are some of the things that your website can help with:

1 Attracting new customers.

2 Enhancing your reputation.

3 Creating revenue streams.

4 Diversifying into new businesses.

5 Learning more about customers.

6 Enhancing print and radio advertising.

7 Increasing referrals.

8 Increasing your profits.

9 Developing brand loyalty.

10 Selling directly.

11 Improving customer service.

These ideas are discussed below together with the website features and the content you'll need to realize them.

Attracting new customers

Your website helps you reach out to potential customers who couldn't find you before: they might come looking for you in search engines, or stumble across a link to your site. Once they're on your website, you have a chance to convert site visitors from all over the world into customers.

Your success depends on how many visitors your site gets and how many of those can be convinced to conduct business with you. Few people will buy on their first visit to a website, so you need to have content on the site that they will return for, giving them time to gain confidence in your business. Send visitors away with an arresting thought, a smile, some software or hot news. But always try to send them away with the thought that your website is worth returning to.

To draw more people in, publish information which potential customers might want to search for on the Internet and make sure that it can be indexed by search engines (see Chapter 9 to learn how they work). This information should be related to your business but not necessarily linked to your sales. While people are reading your articles, you have a chance to tell them about your company and your products so they know where to come when they need them.

If you broaden your website content from telling people about your business to telling readers more about their interests, you create an opportunity for more compelling promotions. Contrast the effectiveness of these two links:

'Click here for Jones & Co Legal Firm'

with

'Click here for a free company legal checklist at Jones & Co'

Here are some ideas for content you can use to attract new customers and remind them to come back.

News and analysis

Your business might already have untapped information flowing through it. If you can capture the news about legislation, trading trends and technologies that passes through your team, you can publish it on your website. You can also publish one-off articles that explain aspects of the industry to newcomers, or update customers on what they might need to know. If you're sending a speaker to an industry event, capture their words and put a transcript or recording on the website.

If the technology behind your products will interest customers, you can write about that or even include a live view of the factory floor using a webcam. Customers shopping for bikes or confectionery might be intrigued to see how they're made, and the article gives you a chance to tell them about your quality controls and what makes your products unique.

Whether people find your information using search engines or links is less important than the fact that it is tightly focused on the interests of your potential customers.

CASE STUDY

Aurora Luggage Limits

US luggage manufacturer Aurora Luggage offers travellers a guide to airline baggage restrictions. Website visitors can check the size and weight restrictions that airlines impose on passengers' checked and carry-on bags depending on the flight carrier, the destination and the type of ticket.

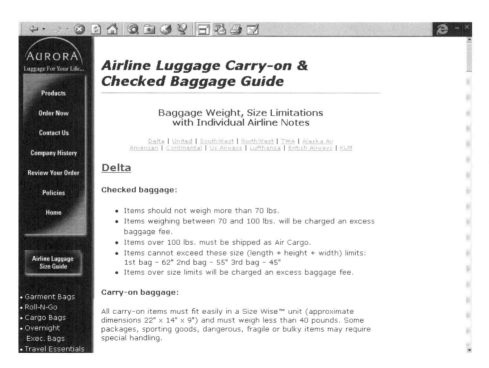

Aurora Luggage's website attracts visitors looking for information on airline luggage restrictions, and gives the company a chance to promote its products to potential customers

Screenshot courtesy Aurora Luggage

Costs associated with excess baggage are shown on the site where available. This enticing content brings visitors on to Aurora Luggage's website where they can browse the company's line of premium luggage and place an order.

The airline guide was promoted with a press release distributed through a newswire service to coincide with the holiday season (see Chapter 9 for ideas on getting press coverage for your website). Aurora Luggage's website is at www.auroraluggage.com.

Print outs

As well as getting a presence on your customer's computer screen, how about getting one on their office noticeboard or fridge door? Create pages that are designed to be printed, and brand them with your website address for a continuous reminder to revisit the site. You'll have more success if your page has a white background and black text. Blocks of colour ravish colour printer cartridges and deter printing.

examples

▶ You could offer troubleshooting tips for software, charts of bird outlines for ornithologists, the periodic table for chemistry students or weight conversion tables for cookery enthusiasts. Think of anything your visitors might need to refer to often while they work or engage in the hobby your business serves.

▶ You could publish a printable calendar including details of important events for your customers.

Make sure that any articles on your site print okay, or have print-friendly versions and that every page includes your contact details and website address.

CASE STUDY

The Midas touch

Children visiting Midas Entertainment's website can print out black and white line drawings of the cartoon dog Midas to colour in. The website promotes the illustrated book *Midas and the Little Red Airplane*. The site has been designed as a safe environment for children, with no links to external websites. As well as the colouring sheets, the site includes games, e-cards, a free screensaver and weekly contests.

'We designed the website so that children can have fun with books and reading,' says Ted Afetian, chief executive officer (CEO) and creator of the Midas book series. 'The Internet has opened up a whole new avenue for small companies, especially self-publishers, to expose their art to the public.'

The website is at www.midaskids.com.

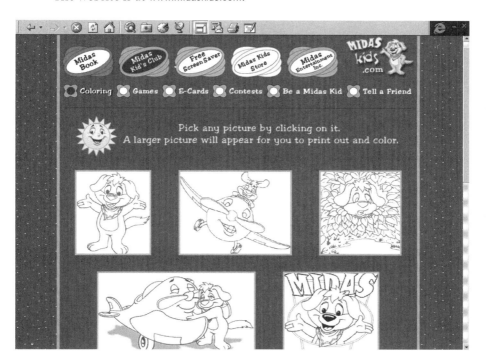

Children visiting Midas Entertainment's website can print off pictures of the cartoon dog Midas which they can colour in

Screenshot ©2000 Midas Entertainment Inc. Used by permission

Shareware

The biggest problem for independent software authors is distribution, which is why they make their software 'shareware'. That means it's free for anyone to copy, distribute and try. But anyone who uses the software after the trial period has to pay a registration fee. It's a low-risk distribution mechanism that enables a lot of software to be released that couldn't compete commercially for shelf space. Freeware is software that you're allowed to copy, try and carry on using without having to pay anyone.

You don't have to pay anything to include shareware and freeware on your website. There is such a wealth of shareware available that there is bound to be something you could offer your visitors – from recipe databases to mathematical modelling programs, music packages to word processors. There are plenty of games too, and you might strike it lucky and find something that touches on themes in your business.

You just need to find the software, put it on your website, and invite people to download it and try it. If it's freeware, you really can give people something for nothing. If it's shareware, you're still doing customers a service by collecting software they'll like (and ideally need) in one place.

Have software checked for viruses before you pass it on and make sure that it's worth downloading. If you pass on obviously broken software or waste download time with programs that don't fulfil their promise, customers will resent you and not just the software author.

You can find shareware all over the Internet, and there are sites dedicated to it at www.download.com and www.shareware.com. The site at www.nonags.com specializes in shareware that doesn't pester users to pay.

Screensavers, wallpapers and skins

Screensavers are programs that start when a computer isn't used for a while and run animations on the display. Their original purpose was to prevent an image getting burned into the monitor, but with today's monitors they're mainly cosmetic.

You can get plenty of freeware screensavers and pass them on, but it's not that hard to have one designed for your company. The screensaver can include a promotional message for your website, but it needs to have something people will want to see on their screen too. You could get some cartoons commissioned or licensed. Animal photos and landscapes are popular if they have a good link with your business (e.g. vets, travel services, motoring services, children's retail). Screensavers that throw up inspiring quotes or jokes can also be tailored nicely to most companies' needs.

There are shareware programs that will create screensavers that slideshow photos or bounce pictures around. Check that the package you choose allows commercial distribution. You could get something custom-programmed for your site, but this can be expensive, so be realistic about how much it will help your business and set a price accordingly.

Screensavers are just one way people can customize their computers. They can change the picture that appears behind their icons and programs (the wallpaper) and can often change the whole look of their software using so-called 'skins'. These skins reshape the program so that while it might do the same job underneath, it looks entirely different. All companies can benefit from getting a relevant (and funny) cartoon commissioned and turning it into wallpaper. Skins are recommended only for companies which know that their customers widely

These are just four of the many skins which users of Freenetmonitor can choose to match the software's appearance to their taste or their mood. The program's function of reporting on the Internet connection speed is unaffected by its appearance. New skins can be downloaded from the website at www.freenetmonitor.com.

Screenshots courtesy of eSynch/Kiss Software Corp

2 Planning your website and creating the content

use a particular piece of skinnable software (such as the Winamp music player or Hotbar, a program that enables users to customize the look of Internet Explorer and which can be downloaded at www.hotbar.com).

As well as attracting visitors, screensavers, skins and wallpaper have the advantage that they remind customers about your website each time they see them.

Product information

Sometimes customers will search the web for information on products they're thinking about buying. If you provide that information, there's a good chance they'll buy it from you when they're ready.

Brochures and technical documentation might be easy to find, but you'll need to redesign them (see Chapter 5 on what makes a good website design). Text split into vertical columns is particularly irritating on screen because readers have to keep scrolling up and down the screen to read it.

Avoid hype and use facts to sell instead. Don't just claim to be the best at something – find a way in which you can prove superiority and use that fact to assert your claim. It helps to use independent reviews or testimonials, especially if you link to them on other known and respected websites (e.g. leading industry magazines).

You can cut the work involved and make the site more of a community by giving customers the chance to review your products. Bitter reviews can still stimulate sales if customers realize they'll like a product for the same features the reviewer hated. This is a powerful strategy for retailers, but companies might be wary of posting negative comments about their own work and might find their supply lines cut by angry manufacturers if they fail to portray products positively.

Enhancing your reputation

If you can become a respected source of information in your industry, it makes it more likely that customers will visit you first when they need to know what's going on. These research visits will spill over into sales and word-of-mouth recommendations of your company.

You can use your website to flaunt your expertise, especially in markets where this is an important part of the service sold, such as in consultancy (publish recent reports), healthcare (give advice on avoiding illness) and accountancy (provide news on taxation online).

If it's going to enhance your reputation, your content must be updated regularly and reliably. Customers need to know they can trust you to tell them what's important as soon as you know. You need to be confident you have the resources to make this commitment. Reputations are tarnished by outdated content.

Nobody's going to respect your content if it's thinly disguised puff for your product line, or if it just slants the news to your company's benefit. Adopt a position of independence and either give your competitors equal prominence in the news or don't mention companies at all.

CASE STUDY

Symantec busts hoax viruses

Companies such as Symantec (www.symantec.com) that make software to defeat computer viruses are a good example of how the Internet can be used to enhance a company's reputation. Several of them have websites that detail the latest virus discoveries, so that people will respect that their software is also being updated regularly.

Symantec's site also reports on hoax viruses, which are scare e-mails warning of bogus viruses. This doesn't help its business directly (you can't protect your computer against an idle threat), but it helps its credibility and gives it more opportunities to promote its commercial products. The company has identified a gap in the information market and filled it, and it doesn't even require it to talk about products at all – neither its own, nor (more importantly) its competitors.

Creating revenue streams

So far the mass market isn't ready to start paying for access to websites, but you might be able to generate subscriptions if you operate within a niche (probably business-to-business) and can deliver something exclusive enough to compete against the free content on other websites. Fees can be justified easily if readers can expect to recoup their investment by acting on your information.

Even if you can't make money by charging users, you might be able to sell space on the website to advertisers. Be careful before making advertising central to your business plan. Revenues are low and it will be difficult to break even unless you have content that will attract the mass market.

The content you choose needs to draw in readers and also keep them for as long as possible so that they can be shown more adverts. While people might tire of reading pages of text, websites that interact with customers will keep them longer, as this case study shows.

CASE STUDY

Fun with Funplanet

Funplanet (www.funplanet.com) in Sweden has found that its games retain visitors for between eight and ten minutes. The company sells advertising space above the games, partnering with other websites which host them and contribute attractive advertising audiences. The game pictured is *Splat the DJ* from a partnership with dance music brand Ministry of Sound.

Funplanet created this game for the Ministry of Sound website where players use the mouse to aim eggs at DJ Fatboy Slim as he pops up on screen

Screenshot courtesy of Funplanet AB

Players use the mouse to aim eggs at the DJs (such as Fatboy Slim shown here), who jump up and down randomly. 'People can get totally absorbed,' says Funplanet's international business manager Mark Williams. 'Before they know it, they've been on the site ten minutes.'

You might also find that a good quality newsletter (preferably about your customers' interests rather than just promoting your product) could attract enough readers to appeal to advertisers. But will these advertisers be your competitors and should you accept their money? See Chapter 6 for more on advertising.

Diversifying into new businesses

Because a lot of the most successful websites have come from start-ups, some managers in small businesses perceive the Internet to be a fertile investment ground. They're encouraged by companies which sell services that depend on customers believing that they too could be millionaires and all they need is the right idea and the right technology.

It can be much easier to set up a new business online than it is off-line, where premises must be rented, travel times impose a tiny catchment area, and sales staff sit idle if customers don't visit for an hour. If you have been planning to enter a new market, the Internet levels the playing field and gives you a chance to compete with the industry leaders head to head.

But before setting up a website unrelated to your core business, consider what will stop richer and more experienced companies from stealing your idea and marketing it more aggressively than you can. In nearly all cases, you will reap a safer and higher return on investment by putting any spare money into your existing business.

Learning more about customers

Customers will reveal much more personal information to you on your website than they would conducting business in a shop or on the phone. If they buy from you, they'll have to tell you their address and contact details. Often they'll answer optional survey questions at the same time.

If they don't buy from you, you might still be able to track which products they look at on the site and which adverts they respond to.

Website visitors will often support simple surveys where they vote for one option from a list. With thought-provoking questions it can become an entertaining feature of the website. As part of the deal, you're expected to tell voters the results of the survey in return for their participation, so beware of competitors getting the inside track on anything valuable.

You can create more detailed online surveys to do more in-depth market research but you can't extend results from the website to the whole of your business. Many of your potential customers won't have access to the Internet or might choose not to visit your website, and these could be your most important customers.

For more accurate customer research, it's much cheaper to contact individual customers by e-mail than it is to write to them or phone them. Don't pester customers with follow-up e-mails, and keep the surveys concise. The greater the time commitment, the less likely it is that customers will take part.

The data you capture through online research can be rough, but it offers many companies their first chance to discover who their customers really are and what they care about.

Chapter 11 discusses measuring website performance and customer behaviour, and Chapter 10 considers the privacy implications.

Enhancing print and radio advertising

With adverts in the phone book and the press, businesses can often only raise awareness that they exist. There isn't space to explain the business's values, or to reassure customers about who works at the firm. Customers are often expected to phone on the basis of a slogan and a company name. And many will be scared of aggressive salesmen or wary of revealing their address to strangers.

These customers might be prepared to investigate your business further, though, by visiting your website. And once they're there, you can reassure them about your business. This is particularly important where companies sell services to consumers (rather than selling to other businesses) and use advertising to reach them.

Here are some ideas for what the site could include.

Company background

Tell readers who they're dealing with and where the company comes from. Tell them which markets you work in and what's important to your business.

How to find us

Provide maps and photos to make it easy for customers to reach you.

Testimonials

Let your success speak for itself. Use comments from previous customers to reassure your future customers. Don't depend on unsolicited praise: ask every customer what they thought of your service and whether they mind being quoted in your promotional materials.

Contact us

Make it easy for customers to get in touch with you: accept letters, e-mails and phone calls. Offer to phone them back at a time that suits them. (See Chapter 8 for more on customer service by e-mail).

Frequently Asked Questions list (FAQ)

This summarizes in question and answer format the company's business and what customers need to know. Use it to address some of the concerns that customers express when approaching you for the first time.

Team news

A page introducing the team with brief profiles and photos helps to make the company approachable. If you have a company newspaper or customer newsletter, you can use a lot of this content on your website. Such publications often report on awards the company has won, staff changes, charity work the company has done, and photo quizzes ('which sales manager did this baby grow up to be?'). Any lighter material should be balanced with factual content so that people can see the company is serious too. Putting team news on the site can also help to win the team's support for the new website.

Webcams

Video cameras can be set up to send images from your workplace to the website regularly (a so-called 'webcam'). Although office cameras can be dull, if you have machinery (e.g. printing press) or craftsmen (e.g. glass-blowing), your visitors might enjoy a real-time view. The best advert for a good entertainment venue (such as a bar or club) is a

2 Planning your website and creating the content

peek inside. You'll need to win the understanding of your team so that they don't feel they're being spied on. You can also use a webcam to provide a view out of the window if you're based somewhere that will interest your potential customers. Webcams also provide novelty value to a website that can make it more memorable for visitors.

CASE STUDIES

The wonders of webcam

Internet Florist arranges the delivery of flowers across the US and has a webcam showing its flower cooler. 'We wanted to use a webcam to demonstrate that we are a real florist,' says manager Michelle Schneider. 'We have been a family-owned florist for over 60 years and have the knowledge and experience to back us up.'

The website was launched in January 1996 and is at www.iflorist.com.

Internet Florist uses its webcam to show that it's a real flower shop

Screenshot courtesy of Internet Florist Association

San Francisco sushi restaurant Ace Wasabi's uses its webcam to show how its sushi is prepared. It sends a powerful signal that the venue has confidence in the quality of its food preparation. The website is at www.acewasabis.com.

See the sushi being prepared before you book your table at Ace Wasabi's

Sreenshot courtesy of Americanese Inc

Increasing referrals

Once the sale is closed, some businesses see their job as over. But many see the opportunity to turn their customers into ambassadors, encouraging them to recommend the product. You can create communities on your site where customers can discuss the product and help each other out. You can also make it easy and fun for customers to recommend the site to their friends. People are more likely to recommend information of interest than particular companies, so see above for ideas on what makes attractive website content.

Communities

People will be more loyal to other people than to any technology. If your site gives them the means to communicate, it will benefit from the through traffic when they return to chat. Potential customers will be drawn by the chance to meet like-minded people on your website and ask them what they think of your service.

Bulletin boards enable people to leave messages for everyone else to read and respond to previous entries. Chatroom visitors can exchange messages only with others who are on the site at the same time. There needs to be a lot of traffic on a site before a chatroom is practical, but specialist bulletin boards are a good way for people to help each other in an industry. With your visitors helping each other, your site develops a rich content base without you needing to research it. It works well where the product or service involves expert knowledge or where the product relates to an interest customers enjoy discussing. Use your customers' passion to convert other customers.

You can tell people what the bulletin board's policy is to deter obscene or inappropriate messages, but you still need to check regularly and delete anything off-topic. If the board strays too far from its intended use, your visitors won't be able to rely on it.

There is the risk that people will criticize your products and services on the bulletin board. You need to be confident that your product and customer service are right, but to pick up occasional glitches, you can invite product complaints at a separate e-mail address with the promise that they can be dealt with more promptly there.

Referral mechanisms

Many websites include features to 'e-mail a friend this page', where readers can enter a friend's e-mail address and a personal message. The content of the page (or sometimes just a link to it) and the recommendation is then e-mailed by the website.

Electronic postcards give website visitors an entertaining way to keep in touch with friends – visitors choose a picture, add a message and enter their friend's e-mail address. The friend receives an e-mail inviting them on to your website to see the picture and read the message together. Electronic postcards bring well-targeted traffic to the site because people will choose images their friends like, and these will be related to your business.

CASE STUDY

A work of art

Artist Hector Duran commissioned a website to promote his design work and is using electronic postcards featuring his illustrations. Visitors who like the pictures can send friends a cheery greeting, and those friends then come to the site to view the picture and hopefully look around the rest of the site.

The site can be seen at www.expressionblue.com and the programming behind the postcards can be licensed for free from www.mypostcards.com.

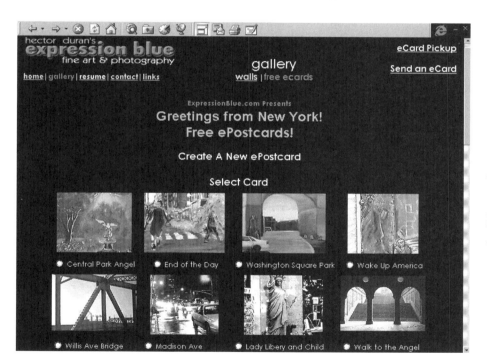

Hector Duran's electronic postcards enable visitors to refer friends to the site

Art by Hector Duran; website design by Nina K DiMaio

Increasing your profits

To be more profitable, you've got to either increase the money that comes into the business or reduce the money you spend. Your website can help you achieve both. Ways to attract new customers and cut the costs of customer acquisition are discussed above. Even if you don't attract any new business, your website can make you more profitable just by lowering costs.

The best thing about using the web to cut costs is that it usually coincides with better customer service. It's cheaper to update a website than a printed brochure and customers benefit too from being able to search for products automatically. It's easier to keep in touch by e-mail than it is by post, and the speed makes it possible to send timely information that customers could never expect of you before.

But this increase in profits needs to be balanced with the cost of creating the site in the first place. Make sure payback periods are realistic. Don't count on your technology lasting more than two years and plan for content to be updated much more often.

Remember that cost-cutting is guaranteed to increase profits only when the value of sales is unaffected. If you migrate your brochure online and refuse to print it, you're more likely to lose money because you'll deter customers who still prefer paper. Don't sacrifice your existing customer base in the hope of future profits. Use the revenue and loyalty they offer to give you leverage in expanding the company through its website.

Developing brand loyalty

The greatest potential to grow a business often lies in increasing the loyalty of existing customers and getting them to buy more. Companies can be forgotten for the months in-between purchases, but building a website enables you to have a relationship with customers all that time. How much more effective would your business be if customers and potential customers were reminded about it every day?

Portal/links page

When most people log on to the Internet they start at their ISP's portal or their favourite search engine. From there they can get the latest news or start looking for what they need. But imagine if they came to you every time they went on to the Internet. What would entice them to do that?

Portal visits might be brief, but you have a chance to push your branding and company message every time your potential customer logs on to the Internet. Include links to bring people into the rest of your site and tease them with headlines to your news stories or special offers in the margins.

Although you're competing with the likes of Microsoft to be their portal of choice, you don't need to be as rich: you just need to create a portal that serves your customers' interests better than a generic gateway does and to persuade them to make it their browser's default homepage.

The trick is to create a web page with enough useful links and tools on it that members of your target audience will always want to start exploring the Internet from there. Don't be blinkered into thinking that only their activities related to your business are important. You must help them meet all their content needs, but that's not as difficult as it sounds. Most search engines are so keen to spread their influence across the Internet that they provide instructions on how to integrate their search engine with your website for free.

By linking to other websites you can provide all the information people need about how they use your product or service, without you having to do any of the work in resourcing it. If you create a good directory catering for your visitors' interests, they will come to your site first in future to do their research online. You can also obtain the latest news headlines to go on your portal (see below).

The sites you link to shouldn't be competitors but should be sites that offer information and products that complement your own. In many cases, you can also get them to link back to bring business to your site too. Think laterally to generate a wide range of links.

example

► A company that makes tents is setting up a website to sell them directly. The site includes a directory of websites related to camping that customers might like, including:

- sites selling maps and guidebooks;
- online mapping and routing websites;
- bicycle shops;
- sites selling weatherproof clothing;
- sites selling mobile computers and mobile phones;
- weather information sites;
- countryside preservation websites;
- easy recipes (for round the campfire);
- websites offering folk music (for campside singalongs);
- holiday photo advice;
- sites selling camping holidays.

To save time researching links, visit www.dmoz.org. You're allowed to use this directory, or any part of it, on your website for free.

Consider offering free e-mail accounts to visitors, but only if you can offer a desirable domain name for the e-mail address to differentiate yourself. Free e-mail accounts are everywhere now and people who want one know where to go. There's little chance of them stumbling across your site in the search. It's more of an added bonus for regular visitors than a feature likely to attract visitors.

Selling directly

Bus timetables, long-distance phone charges, the weather and your opening hours can all have a negative effect on your business. You can never know how many sales you're losing through near-random influences like this, but your website gives you a means to shatter many of the barriers customers face when buying from you by phone or in person. You can accept orders online and dispatch them by post to make sales, however remote your premises might be.

Sometimes competitors are able to use contracts or informal agreements to freeze you out of markets or make it difficult for your business to compete. If your competitors have a strong influence on your distribution channels, the Internet gives you a valuable chance to start again.

Even if you are a manufacturer and already have retail distribution, you can increase your margins by selling directly. Be careful that this doesn't turn your existing distribution chain against you, though. You'll be making competitors of your partners as you both try to sell the same products from the web.

If you're going to increase sales, make sure first that you can handle them. If you're already running at full capacity, extra orders will mean expanding the team or the machinery of your business, which might be too risky. You might also need to consider delivery for the first time and will need to resource this.

See Chapter 7 for more on selling from your website.

Improving customer service

One criticism of supermarkets is that they don't offer the personalized service that good local stores do, where the grocer greets visitors by name and remembers what products they like.

But on the web you can personalize the service that customers receive and combine it with the economies of scale of mass marketing. Information can be published cheaply and web pages can be tailored to the customers' preferences automatically.

If you compete on service, you don't have to compete on price.

Here are some ideas for how your website might help you improve customer service.

Personalized products

Now that the web is enabling customers to deliver orders in a structured form, products as diverse as clothing, books, toys and sandwiches can be tailored to the customer's wishes on demand. The line between consumers and producers is blurring, with customers choosing the components in their Dell computer, or auditioning songs and arranging them for a customized CD. The factory machinery produces the product, but the customer tells it what to do and gets a result that better fits their needs.

CASE STUDY

Customizing with Booktailer.com

Don't want to carry a bulky travel guide on holiday, padded with suggestions for places you'd hate to visit? Booktailor.com lets you pick and choose the content you want from different publishers and different destinations to make a travel book that fits your interests and your itinerary better.

Readers tell the website where they're going and when they're travelling and can then choose to include chapters from different publishers

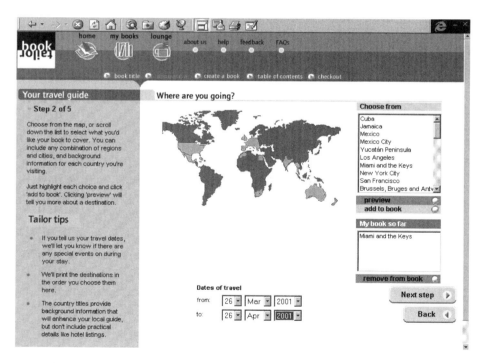

Booktailor's website enables customers to choose chapters from different travel publications which are then compiled into a customized holiday guide, which is printed and sent by post

Screenshot © Booktailor Ltd

covering accommodation, culture, entertainments, shopping and history among others. The book can even include information on local events during the holiday. The chapters are automatically printed and compiled into a ring-bound book which is sent by post.

Product recommendations

If Jean and Chas both buy the same product, it's a good bet that any other products Jean buys, Chas might also like. Sophisticated systems that automatically recommend products based on what else a customer has bought can be expensive, but you can easily keep track of which product types people like (e.g. rock music, pop music, blues) and when they last visited, and tell them what's new in their preferred section. You can even ask customers to describe themselves so that you can improve their experience at the site.

When applied to frequently purchased goods, recommendation systems also make it inconvenient for customers to switch allegiance. If your website remembers their last shopping list and they just have to add this week's new items and delete those they don't need to buy again, they can cut the time taken to minutes. If they go to another website, they have to teach that supplier all about their tastes and shopping behaviour.

Don't scare your customers by using data they don't know you're collecting. Respect their privacy and explain the benefits. They won't be impressed if you start telling them they need to buy toilet paper and they haven't allowed you to use this information. Give customers the chance to opt out of any data collection so that you don't lose customers who don't like the idea.

After-sales care

Using your website, you can provide customers with any information they might need whenever they need it. There are no manuals for you to print (or for customers to lose) and the information is delivered cheaply and promptly.

If your product is technical (a washing machine, perhaps), you could provide detailed instructions in a range of languages, and segment them for the convenience of customers with different levels of experience. Furniture assembly brochures need to show exploded views, but imagine the impact of a 3D model on your website that the customer could rotate and magnify at all stages of assembly. Even if you are only retailing the product, you should take responsibility for your customer's satisfaction with it. It is your business that will be tarnished by a poor shopping experience, not just the manufacturer's.

CASE STUDY

Getting technical

RS Components (www.rs-components.com) uses its website to provide detailed technical information on the thousands of electronic components it supplies. Customers are spared the inconvenience of archiving technical data sheets on the kit they use, and have the convenience of the information being a click away when they need it.

Although manuals and telephone help are far from redundant (the Internet is not yet available everywhere), cutting the number of puzzled inquiries will usually cut costs and increase profits too.

Faster turnaround for technical queries

You might be able to manage e-mailed queries more easily than phone calls. E-mails can be stored and answered in a batch, whereas telephones need to be staffed all the time. You can also get customers to complete online forms so that you can guide them in providing any data you need to be able to help them. See Chapter 8 for more on this.

Secure communications

Many businesses have information on their clients that could be abused if it fell into the wrong hands. Using your website, you can provide a secure means for customers to send you computer files for the first time. Customers won't need any special encryption software, but the data will be scrambled if anyone intercepts it on its way through the Internet.

Immediate product delivery

Newspapers and CDs are just wrapping for the words, pictures and music we want to buy. If your product is more about the information than the materials, perhaps it can be delivered online. Other examples include sewing patterns, maps, books, photographs, software and paintings. All these can be sent as files over the Internet without the cost of physical manufacture and distribution and without the hassle of going to the shops or waiting for the post.

Admittedly, quality can be a problem with Internet delivery. People like to see the texture on paintings and might want their sewing patterns printed on paper too big or too flimsy for desktop printers to accommodate. Many customers don't have fast enough Internet access yet to fully unleash the potential for delivering some products. But some of these concerns will fade, and others will open opportunities to segment the market. Lower-quality digital versions of some products can be sold, with the original non-Internet product being available at a premium.

CASE STUDY

Move it with Bustamove.com

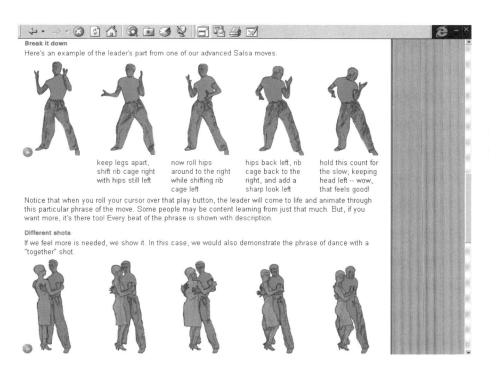

Learn to dance by downloading lessons that combine animation with text from Bustamove's website

Screenshot courtesy of Bustamove Inc

The web makes it easy for people to communicate with each other, exchanging text, pictures, sound and cartoons cheaply. This makes it an ideal channel for delivering some types of teaching that were delivered face-to-face before.

Bustamove.com was set up by Jeffrey Grossman and Kate Moschandreas to sell dance tuition over the web. Lessons include animated illustrations to show the moves and detailed explanations of the timing, stance and potential mistakes of each move.

Round-the-clock service

Long after you've gone to bed your website is still working. Whenever customers are curious about your product range, or whichever time zone they are based in, your website will provide them with information on demand. And you can take credit card orders when customers feel like buying and don't have to rely on them returning when you're open.

Search boxes

Customers can get information on demand – whatever they want, whenever they want it. Include a search facility on every page of your site if it has enough information to justify it. But make sure that it's sensibly indexed and the list of results is easy to understand.

Offering accounts

Let customers open an account with you. They'll be spared the worry of sending their credit card details over the Internet for each purchase, and they'll be saved the time of giving you their address each time.

Charting a strategy

To plot a strategy for your website, you'll need to pick and mix the ideas above. If you want to use the site to increase referrals from your existing customer base, for example, you'll need to give them a reason to visit the site in the first place and that might mean creating a portal or putting tutorials online. Wallpaper might attract visitors, but it's also a powerful memory-jogger for customers who download it.

You must be clear about how your website will help grow your company. Only then can you choose content that supports that aim.

Planning your content

Once you know what content you need, you're ready to think about how it will be created. Some website features can be licensed for free, but your website designers might be more likely to recommend their own (and non-free) alternatives if you don't ask for free ones.

When writing the content for your website, you'll need to keep it snappy and put it in global context, as shown below.

© Nik Scott Illustrations. www.nikscott.com

Using syndicated content and free website enhancements

Minutes after they've happened, news of the latest world or industry events could be reaching your customers through your website. Your site could carry a box of the latest headlines which take visitors to the full story when clicked. It's free content you couldn't possibly resource yourself and you can pick and choose the publications you want to work with.

CASE STUDY

Harvesting the headlines

You can get free news feeds for your website from www.moreover.com. The company indexes news and information headlines from more than 1,800 sources all over the web and delivers them to websites as blocks of headlines dedicated to a particular industry or interest. There are 800 pre-selected categories, but websites can define their own keywords to have news delivered to order. By inserting a few lines of code into your website, you can have the current news harvested and pushed to your page.

Moreover.com offers this service to demonstrate its products for gathering business intelligence for companies that want to check what's being published about them, their competitors or their industry online. This screenshot shows how the headlines appear fully integrated with the host website.

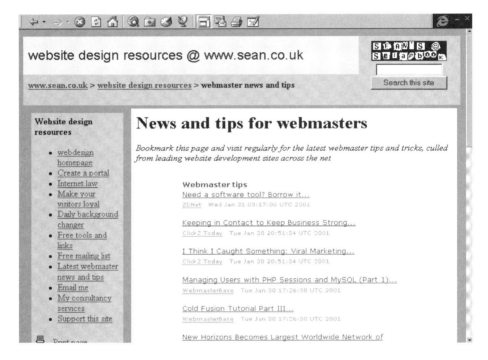

Moreover provides free headline feeds which businesses can build into their website

Screenshot courtesy of Moreover

Syndication is a good way to add extra content to a website, but it's not a good idea to depend on it for content that is essential to your site's success unless you have a watertight contractual arrangement to protect its availability.

Your site must build on free content and offer something exclusive as well, otherwise your visitors will cut you out and go straight to your source after you've introduced them.

There are a lot of free tools for maintaining postcards, polls, chat-rooms and bulletin boards. Some of these ask you to carry adverts on the page they give you in exchange for using the services. Often they let you rent an advert-free version.

There's no need to reinvent the wheel, but make sure that the tools you use are a good fit with your design. Ideally you want the colours to match your own site and for the page to carry your logo and navigation. It's essential that there's a clear link back to your website from any external pages you use. (See Chapter 5 for more guidance on site design.)

Beware of any risk transfer in the contract terms. Some of the usage contracts for free site services make you liable for the actions of your website visitors. If someone used your bulletin board to send a pirated music file, for example, you might find that the bulletin board provider could recover all their legal costs from you if the record company took them to court. If you can't find an alternative, it might be cheaper to have something custom written, rather than get it for 'free' and not be able to control the cost of dispute resolution. (See Chapter 10 for more legal tips.)

How to write for the web

Screen space and reader attention spans are limited, so don't waffle. Many companies proudly stamp 'Established 1832' or something similar on their brochures and then go on to describe the company's birth. Be frank and ask yourself whether your customers care. You need to tell them what they do want to know straight away.

Good website content is customer-focused. Talk about the user benefits of your products, not features. Deliver information they'll like and don't make them wade through promotional puff. Use facts, not hype, to push products.

And write concisely. That doesn't mean you can't be creative, but you need to make sure that you don't repeat the same idea in different sentences and don't use more words than necessary. Some words can be deleted altogether, such as 'really', 'actually' and 'very'. You're trying to communicate, not astound the audience with your vocabulary, so stick to short words that are easy to digest. Here are some waffly words to look out for, together with shorter alternatives:

a large number of – many

a large proportion of – much

accommodation – hotel/home

additional – more

adjacent to – next to

along with – with

ameliorate – improve

approximately – about

are able to – can

at this moment in time – now

behind schedule – late

come on stream – launch/start

demonstrate – show

donate – give

during the course of – during

endeavour – try

finalize – confirm

frequently – often

in order to – to

in short supply – scarce/rare

in spite of the fact that – despite

in view of the fact that – because

negotiations – talks

was a witness of – saw

in the vicinity of – near

remuneration – pay

utilize – use

Make sure that your writing is accurate. It doesn't have to follow the obscure rules of grammar (such as never ending a sentence with a preposition), but it makes your website look amateur if it breaks basic rules or misspells words. Be careful with words such as 'there' ('their', 'they're') and 'here' ('hear') which have different spellings depending on the meaning. Be consistent in the formatting of dates and the choice of spelling where it's optional.

A wall of text is intimidating, so let it breathe with frequent paragraph breaks. Stick to one idea per paragraph.

The writing is one of the most important jobs on your website development, so make sure it's allocated to someone who writes accurately and clearly. Consider hiring a copywriter to write your content or to smarten up your articles.

Customers can rarely judge the quality of your goods or services by looking at your website, but they will notice how much care you've invested in your copy. If a company can't be bothered to check spellings, what are the chances it will offer great customer service?

Checklist: writing for international readers

Now you're online, you're a global player. Don't confuse customers, and miss business, by writing ambiguously. Use this checklist.

- Have you made it clear which towns, states or countries you can supply to? A pizza shop, for example, doesn't want to get an order they'll need to put a moped on a plane to deliver. And remember that city names aren't always unique, as these examples show:

  Athens: Greece or USA?

  Birmingham: UK or USA?

  Brest: France or Former Soviet Republic?

  Hastings: New Zealand or UK?

  Saint John's: Antigua or Canada?

  St. Petersburg: Russia or USA?

  Toledo: Spain or USA?

  Victoria: Australia or Canada?

  Worcester: UK or USA?

Beware too of using words or phrases such as 'regional', 'local' or 'the country's best' which are irrelevant to global visitors.

example

► A fast-food outlet might use this message on its home page: 'We deliver in one hour to your home in Birmingham, Alabama, USA.' Visitors in the wrong Birmingham don't need to waste any more time on the site and Americans are reassured about the delivery terms and area.

■ Have you explained which currency your prices are in? Many countries (including the US, Canada, Australia and Hong Kong) use the dollar, so it's best to indicate the country as well as the currency. Explain that although you'll bill customers US$15, for example, their credit card company will convert it and charge them in their home currency. You can provide approximate rates for main foreign markets and link to online currency converters to help them out.

■ If you're going to offer translations, don't assume readers come from the most obvious country for that language. French is spoken widely throughout Africa and English is a popular second language for business. For that reason, it's better to use language names than flags or maps on navigation buttons.

■ Have you checked that dates are clear? In the US the date 5/11/07 would be read as 11 May 2007 but in Europe that same date means 5 November 2007.

■ Have you checked that any references to times include the time zone? You might be able to cut confusion by also making the website display the current time in your country.

example

► An online bookshop might say: 'Come back at 17:00 EST for a web chat with best-selling author Frank Madeupname (the time here is now 15:37 EST).'

■ If you're closing to celebrate Christmas, Thanksgiving, Chinese New Year or any other festival, have you made it clear on the site when this holiday is and when the business will be responding to e-mails again?

- Have you checked for seasonal references? While Europeans might hope to build snowmen in December, Australians will be on the beach. It's clearer to say a product launches in quarter three next year than say it's coming out 'next autumn'.

- Have you had any translations checked by native language speakers? Automatic translation software might be able to look up words, but it can't understand what you intended them to mean. You might want to link to an automatic translation website as a service to visitors, but make sure its limits are clear so you aren't blamed for its shortcomings. Automated services can't understand what words mean in context and provide at best a crib sheet for those who already know some of the foreign language. Visit this book's website at www.sbwtw.com to try one out.

- Have you checked that you're not localizing the website unnecessarily? It might seem helpful to include weather forecasts to help your local customers, but will it deter new foreign clients?

- Phone numbers, postal codes and addresses are formatted differently and are of a different length in different countries. Have you checked that any forms allow foreign visitors to enter their details in full, and don't assume there's a fault if their entries are longer or shorter than you might expect from your own country?

Integrating your website with your business

When the competition comes from Internet start-ups that have secured millions in venture capital, it might look like they're in the strongest position. But they often don't have the premises or established customer relationships that you do. Bookshops are already focusing on the experience of shopping, letting customers read the books in comfort and setting up coffee shops. You could put a computer kiosk in your store or office, using your website's architecture. Your kiosk might help people sample your product or find similar products they like and then refer them to a shelf to pick one up, or offer to ship it direct from the website.

As Chapter 9 reveals, your team members will often have the best chance to promote your website, so involve them now. Ask them how the website could make their jobs easier and improve the service customers receive.

Summary

Although you can outsource much of your website's development, its strategic direction must come from within the company. There are many ways that a website can help your company to grow, but these will depend on your position in the marketplace and your industry. You'll need to have text, photos and interactive website features that support your aim.

Think beyond putting your brochure online. Good content attracts visitors and makes it easier to promote the website, but doesn't necessarily push products. It gives readers a reason to visit the site, giving you a chance to do business with them and fulfil your website's purpose.

Your content mix needs to be unique and well targeted at your audience's interests. That doesn't mean it has to be expensive – you can throw free content and cheap plug-ins into the mix and can often draw on your own or team members' expertise.

Everything on your website needs to be accurate and written for an international audience.

Your website's success depends on what it has to say and how it says it, so it's important that you articulate your goals to your website designers to make sure that they understand not just what you're putting on your website but what you want that to achieve. It will improve the relevance of their suggestions.

Resourcing your website design

It's unlikely you would employ an amateur website designer on a salary as high as yours, but that is what happens if you fail to delegate the job

Introduction

Now that you know how your website will help grow your business, and you know what content you want it to deliver, you're ready to think about who's going to build it and what that's going to cost.

There are four ways to resource the website design:

- Design it yourself.
- Get a friend to do it.
- Commission an outside agency to design it.
- Develop it in-house.

As the following graph shows, the more tightly you need to control the website, the more it's going to cost. As the rest of this chapter reveals, however, that doesn't mean you have to go with the most expensive option.

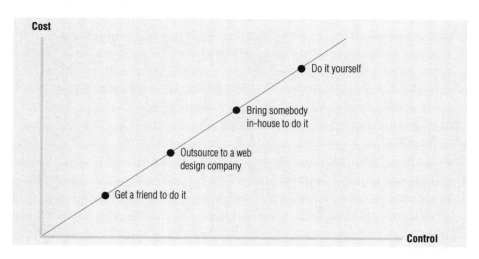

How the control you have over your website is related to the cost of your design team

The importance of delegation

Website design used to be for geeks only, but programs as easy to use as word processors now enable anyone to create sites. With the technical barriers dissolving, it's tempting to take on the job of building your company's website yourself. But the learning curve is no less steep now than it ever was – although new software can make it easier to solve the technical challenges in website design, the packages do nothing to help users understand graphic design, organising computer files or how to make websites easy to use. These are key to a website's success. The site design programs do what you want, but the real skill is knowing what's a good idea, and that comes with experience. Like electronic musical instruments, these software packages can be powerful tools in the right hands, but they don't transform beginners into experts.

Consider what you'd need to learn to design your own site:

- how to use a package that creates websites, such as Dreamweaver or Frontpage;
- how to lay out a website;
- how to organise and link documents;
- how to design graphics;
- how to set up shopping carts and secure website software;
- how to test the website, following every link and verifying every page, making sure it will work on different computers and browsers;
- how to optimize the site design for rapid download;
- how to register domain names, secure certificates, etc.;
- how to put your website files on the server for public access;
- new technologies and design trends as they arise.

It's not that this is difficult, especially since you might already have many of the skills involved. The problem is that it's more expensive for you to design your own site than it is for you to buy in appropriate skills. The difference is that the cost is hidden if you do it yourself.

If you are a sole trader, you can multiply the amount of time you're likely to spend by your hourly rate to work out the real cost of developing the site yourself. That time could otherwise be spent earning money directly, or attending clubs and meetings to generate more work.

If you already have a team and work as a manager, your time would be better spent on expanding the business and working on its future strategy. It's unlikely you would employ an amateur website designer on a salary as high as yours, and yet that is exactly what happens if you fail to delegate the job.

Experienced designers will work more quickly than you, so a higher hourly rate than your own need not deter you. If they charge twice as much and take half the time, you're still breaking even. And the result will be better than anything you would have achieved alone.

Designing a website yourself gives you most control over it, but it's expensive and you're limited to your skills and how quickly you can extend them.

The pros and cons of designing your own website

Advantages	Disadvantages
Might have spare time anyway	Steep learning curve
You might find it enjoyable	Results can look amateurish
No cash outlay	Poor use of your time
You keep absolute control over the complete site	Responsibility for everything on the complete site
	Burden of keeping up with new design trends
	Burden of keeping site updated gets in the way of core business or means the site is neglected

Getting a friend to design the site

One of the cheapest ways to get a website is if a friend or relative offers to do it for you. Many people now have the technical skills required to design sites and are eager to create a portfolio to help them break into the design industry. People at this level in the industry can be talented because they've taught themselves the creative tricks out of a love of the technology and a need to prove themselves rather than any professional duty. Your friend will be enthusiastic and will have a personal stake in the site's success.

If they have an understanding of your business, you won't need to manage the site development too closely either. It can be expensive to change plans when working commercially, but a friend might be more tolerant of adjustments.

The arrangement's flexibility is also its weakness. You have no control over timescales or quality. You can't govern when the site is designed, and you are in a poor position to enforce deadlines. Your friend won't sacrifice their social life for the project, so it will be squeezed into slack days and weekends, like a hobby.

Quality can also be a problem. If the site's being designed as a favour, you'll find it difficult to be brutally critical if it doesn't meet the goals or presentation standards you set the business. Before going ahead, check your friend's previous websites for any of the design crimes listed in the checklist in Chapter 5 to see whether you're likely to get an amateur-looking result.

If there's no portfolio to look at, don't let your company website become an experiment by making it your friend's first project. The main resource you need to acquire is experience in designing sites.

Although websites are often priced for the initial design, most of the cost to you will be in updating and ongoing maintenance. If you don't have an agreement that covers support throughout the website's life, you're going to need to find someone else to take it over later. It's better to find someone who will be able to build the site and tailor future amendments.

If your friend is good at designing sites, you are confident they will be available for ongoing support, and your friendship can take the strain, formalize your working relationship and offer some compensation. Once you have a business relationship, you can be more open with criticism and your friend is motivated to allocate time to you promptly.

The pros and cons of getting a friend to design your website

Advantages	Disadvantages
Free or cheap	No control mechanism
Enthusiastic	Results can appear amateurish
Sometimes extremely talented	Delay because the project is a low priority for designer
Sometimes low management time needed	Low level of ongoing support
	Can't be too critical because of hurt feelings

Outsourcing the website design

For most companies, outsourcing the site design to another company is the best option.

When you partner with an outside company to develop your site, your success depends partly on theirs. If the company thrives, its skills will grow organically as new people join the team, so 'your' webdesign team keeps pace with technology changes. If the company fails, though, the life of your investment will be cut short and you'll have to start over with another company learning how the website works or creating it afresh.

You have a strong control mechanism because the design agency won't get paid if it doesn't deliver, and because it's their core business webdesign companies will offer relatively fast turnaround times. On the other hand, the agency gets more money if it can market more services to you so you need to keep your business vision firmly in focus to ensure its suggestions will help your company.

Because an external design team has little contact with your company (and none with many departments), you'll need to communicate your key values and the website's business goals. Keep your designers informed of how your business is changing. The quality of your design team's advice will reflect your ability to communicate your aims to them.

Look at previous sites the company has designed when its sales staff are pitching for your business, but remember that you're not buying their old ideas: you're looking for new ideas that will help your company. If they don't seem willing or able to discuss the potential of your company online, you're better off looking for another firm. Make sure that previous sites have good designs (see Chapter 5), or be confident that you can brief the design team on what you would want changed for your site.

Many companies now provide a quick service to get a business online, using design templates and pasting in your documents. Working like this is a bit like a toymaker designing games to fit stockpiled cardboard boxes, but part of what you buy is a service customizing the templates. If you just want to create a small brochure site, this can be a good option. But don't spend much money on a site that's just a few pages of text, and make sure that you don't compromise on good design (again, see Chapter 5). Be warned too that companies running quick and easy operations might not be able to support your more ambitious plans later.

The pros and cons of outsourcing the website design to an agency

Advantages	Disadvantages
The skills at your disposal are updated as the company grows	The control mechanism is financial, so you'll have to make sure that meeting your business goals is rewarded financially
You can draw on a broader base of skills	You are dependent on their success
Faster turnaround time	
Greater wealth of experience in developing websites than through alternative options	

Getting the site designed in-house

If your Internet investment is going to be significant, it might be better to bring someone into the company and divert the money that might have gone to a webdesign company to their salary and the equipment needed to design the site. If your website technology (rather than the content) is crucial to your business success, it's essential. If you're competing on innovation, you can't invest in a team of mercenaries who could be recruited to work for your competitors at the same time as working for you.

Your in-house website designer will be immersed in the company culture and will know what's going on all the time, making it easier to use initiative in steering the website. You'll have complete control over when updates are done, and will be able to control development through normal staff incentives.

The website also has a focal point inside the company: an ambassador to sing its virtues to other departments and someone to welcome suggestions or problems and make sure they are followed up. If you find the right person, you'll be able to delegate some responsibility for making sure that the site meets the business goals rather than just assigning the design work to them.

To keep your website designers, you'll need to reward them well and give them challenging opportunities. Be prepared for them to leave to join a richer global company by ensuring that their work is well documented so that successors can understand how the website works.

If you've got someone on the team already who's keen to design the site, make sure that they're up to a professional standard before giving them the job. And don't forget to allocate time and money for training so that your team can keep up with advances in technology.

The pros and cons of building an in-house design team

Advantages	Disadvantages
Excellent control	Difficult to keep skills up to date – need to allocate time to training
Fast communications	Designers are often tempted away to other companies by better offers, especially from small businesses where their creative scope will be limited
Continuity control through documentation and handover periods	Upfront investment in the hardware, software and staff costs to create the site can be prohibitive for small businesses
Low management time needed	
Control of proprietary technology	
Potentially strong links throughout company and understanding of company culture	
Website has an ambassador in-house to promote the site to the rest of the company and to customers	

Getting the balance right

Most small businesses need to recruit another company to do the website design. But even then, they should appoint a manager inside the company who can take responsibility for the site. Don't let the site's success depend on what little time senior managers can give it if there is a team that can take on the day-to-day running. Make sure that everyone in the business understands the website's goals so that any work the team does harmonizes with the site's aims.

If you're a sole trader, don't over-commit yourself. Create a site that won't distract you from your core business more often than you can afford.

What's it going to cost?

If you're committed to having a profitable website, this is where you can guarantee it happens. You can cut your costs to match your expected income and scale the site up as the business grows.

If you have more confidence in your business plan, splash out for higher potential returns. Websites (like companies) stagnate without investment and the chances are your business wouldn't exist today if there hadn't been some lucky gambles in the past.

You can get a basic website for less than the cost of the computer you'll view it on, but interactive and animated websites will cost more. Prices vary wildly for website design services and it's not always the case that you get what you pay for. The industry hasn't been around long enough to settle down to standard prices, so interview potential designers to check they understand what you need and that they can deliver it.

Design companies usually charge by the hour. Don't be put off by high or low hourly rates – a more expensive designer might take half the time and cost the same as a slower, cheaper designer. You can often persuade them to work to a fixed budget for the whole site design, but they might build in some slack in their price to cover any re-work that is necessary through your corrections or their misunderstanding of the time needed.

To get an idea of what the website is worth to you, consider how you expect the site to increase your profits. If you're hoping to cut costs with your site, your potential savings set a ceiling for the website budget. If you're planning to get customers to buy more or shop with you more often, or you're hoping to bring in new customers, it's more difficult to estimate the benefit, but you'll notice if you're wildly out of step. Remember, don't spend thousands on a site that's only ever going to bring in hundreds.

Make sure that you consider the lifecycle cost of the project as well. Your website will need regular maintenance and periodic redesigns, so find out how much updates are going to cost. Never forge a ten-year plan to recoup your website costs. A lifespan of two years for a site design would be optimistic.

You'll also need to consider the costs of:

- creating content;
- your management time;
- hosting the website (see Chapter 4);
- promoting the website (see Chapter 9).

Checklist: the brief to designers

Whether you're briefing an internal or external team, you'll need to make sure that they're clear on what the site aims to do and how you'll work together. These are the issues you'll need to discuss:

- the site's purpose (who you want to attract to the site, what you want them to do there, and how it will help your business);
- the site's proposed content (type and quantity and relative importance – see Chapter 2 for more on content;
- how the content will be organized (see Chapter 5 for more on designing your website's navigation);
- how the content will be delivered (it's often cheaper to provide designers with text on a disk than on paper);
- how often content will be updated;

- the desired look of the site;

- the importance of speed-optimized site design (see Chapter 5);

- timescales for site completion, together with deadlines for you to supply content;

- who will update the content and how;

- the technology used to create the site and what documentation will be available for other designers to use if the site maintenance changes hands;

- which computers and software the site must work on (see Chapter 5);

- the cost of site development;

- the cost of maintenance (site design updates);

- the cost of content updates;

- copyright (you'll need to make sure you get the copyright in the design you buy for any uses you need to make of the site. See Chapter 10 for more on copyright);

- who is in charge of the website design within your company;

- how much freedom is being delegated to designers, and what decisions they need to refer back to your website manager.

Summary

There are several ways to resource the design of your website which show a compromise between cost and control.

The best solution is to get an outside agency to do it for you unless you are investing enough to justify bringing someone into the company. You should still aim to delegate responsibility for the website within your company and if that's impractical you need to scale the website back to something you can maintain reliably.

The checklist in this chapter can be used to ensure that you've discussed the important issues with your design team before they put finger to keyboard.

Chapter 5 shows how you can evaluate the quality of design you see in designers' portfolios and in their proposals for your online presence.

Don't forget that as well as recruiting website designers and their equipment if they're in-house, you'll need to resource the creation of content (see Chapter 2), the site administration (paperwork such as domain name renewals and secure certificates) and the site promotion (see Chapter 9).

Naming and hosting your website

The real value of a domain name rests in its promotion and the goodwill the underlying website has attracted

Introduction

Now that you know how your website will contribute to your business, what content it will carry and who will design it, you're ready to think about what it's going to be called and how it will be hosted.

This chapter will tell you the value of a domain name, how to pick one and what you need to ask your techies about the server.

The value of a domain name

A domain name is the part of the website address that tells the browser which server to go to for the pages the visitor wants. You need to buy a domain name, a '.com' of your own around which you can build your website. It is your guarantee of ongoing traffic and of a return on your investment in promoting the website.

Many Internet service providers will give you space for your website for free and there are plenty of companies bartering webspace in exchange for your site carrying their adverts. If you used one of these services, your website address would be something like this:

- www.yourcompanyname.serviceprovider.com or
- www.serviceprovider.com/yourcompanyname or
- www.serviceprovider.com/~yourcompanyname (the worst: even experienced typists will have to hunt for the squiggly tilde character).

But an address like this makes you dependent on your hosting company. All your traffic goes through their domain name, so your website is merely a bolt-on to theirs. What if the hosting company goes bust, or changes its terms unfavourably? If you move the site, visitors won't know where to go, incoming links will be broken and bookmarks won't work. You'll have to start again to promote the site from nothing. As long as your website address is based on another company's domain name, you run this risk.

Buying your own domain name gives you independence. You can move the site to a different server and keep the same website address so that all incoming links and bookmarks still work uninterrupted. With domain names being so cheap to buy, businesses look risky and unprofessional if they haven't made that investment. It shows a lack of commitment to the site.

Internet myth domain names are expensive

Domain names based on adding .com to dictionary words or celebrity names are often sold at a premium because people might just type in that domain name to see where it leads.

But if you look at the most popular websites and the best known web businesses, very few of them have domain names that you might conceivably type in on the off-chance that you'd find what you want. Some of them are decidedly obscure:

- Hotmail (e-mail)
- Yahoo (a directory of websites)
- Amazon (books)
- Ebay (auctions)
- Geocities (a community of free websites).

The real value of a domain name rests in its promotion and the goodwill the underlying website has attracted. Your domain name becomes a brand name, and until you've exposed it to the marketplace and built up a flow of traffic, it's worthless.

There are companies that rush out and register domain names they don't need so they can sell them at a premium to people who do need them. But since the value of a domain name depends on what you do with it and not what it is, you shouldn't spend a lot of money on a domain name for a small business.

Domain names expire if the subscription isn't renewed and this can bring highly memorable names back on to the market. But it's risky to buy pre-owned domain names. Visitors will arrive with expectations of what's at the site and how much they trust it. You'll eventually have to pay more for your server if your visitor traffic is high and how will you be able to tell your customers from those who were looking for the old (and possibly unrelated) business? Buying an expired domain name might seem like traffic for nothing, but you only need to attract visitors that will conduct business with you or will become regular visitors if you're selling adverts on the site.

Picking a domain name

The obvious choice is to add '.com' to your business name, but that will be memorable only for existing customers and might lead to unnecessarily long domain names. Be creative. If your website is using articles to attract visitors, choose a domain name that reflects the site's purpose and its content rather than something based on your business name. The address will be more appealing to visitors when they see your link and they will remember it more easily than the name of a company they've never heard of.

Rarely will you have your first choice of domain name. Although you can register trade marks within your industry, the trade marking system recognizes 42 product categories. This means there could be 42 products with the same name, but just the one '.com' domain name and that goes to whoever is quickest in registering it. If someone else already has your desired domain name and is using it for legitimate business, there's not much you can do about that. If somebody has registered it and is hoarding it in the hope of selling it to you, you might be able to take legal action. In practice, it's probably cheaper to pay them off and much cheaper to just think up a new domain name.

Here are some tips on picking domain names.

- Have a short, memorable website address and remind customers what it is by including it prominently in the website design.

- Avoid domain names that have any words embedded in them that could be seen to be rude. Obscenity filters have prevented people from accessing Beaver University's homepage in the US and any content at all to do with the UK town of Scunthorpe.

- Include words related to the business or content in the domain name. If your business is flowers, putting the word 'flowers' in the domain name can help prioritize the site on some search engines.

- Avoid using hyphens and don't use domain names that need them to be readable. If you do need to use hyphens, register the versions of the domain names that don't include hyphens as well. Visitors can't remember hyphenated addresses as easily, and if the non-hyphenated version of your name is owned by another site, it will get a lot of your repeat visitors.

- Consider registering probable mistypings of your domain name. If you have a popular site, people could hijack your traffic just by setting up a domain name based around a likely mistyping of your domain name. This is important only if you have a renowned brand name you're putting online.

- Register your brand names as domain names. Make these domain names take visitors to a section on your main site, so that you pick up the business if a customer enters the address experimentally but don't incur the cost of promoting multiple websites.

- Don't try to acquire all the names you (or your competitors) would have liked. It might be tempting to try to freeze out the competition by taking all the good names, but they'll just get another name and you'll be paying for names you're not using and hogging scarce Internet resources.

- Pick a name that you can easily tell people on the telephone. Avoid difficult or ambiguous spellings.

Domain name extensions

Commercial domains usually end in .com. Some of the other extensions available include .org for organizations and .net for networks. In November 2000, seven additional extensions were approved, including .biz for businesses, .pro for professionals such as accountants, doctors and lawyers, and .aero for the aviation industry. It's worth checking whether an extension for your industry has been released yet or is expected soon.

There are also national suffixes, such as .co.uk for UK companies, .de for Germany (Deutschland) and .fr for France. These national suffixes (especially .to for Tonga) are sometimes used to finish off words or phrases, the first half of which is the domain name. This is best avoided because the full stop in the middle of a word can be confusing.

Websites with regional extensions look like national companies. If your international business is limited to export, it might make sense to use a national extension, but bear in mind that many companies find the Internet gives them a chance to go global for the first time. If trading internationally, you should register both your national name and your .com domain to prevent any confusion if somebody else acquires the one you're not using. They can still point to the same website, but you should focus promotion on the .com version.

The extensions available are being increased all the time, so it is too expensive to try to defend your brand across all of them. Large companies have goodwill invested in their brand names that others might try to hijack and some buy all the domain names based on their trade marks to prevent this. Few small companies face a similar risk and few can afford to spend tens of thousands of dollars acquiring domain names defensively. It's best to buy domain names you need and tackle any trade mark infringements as they occur.

Big firms sometimes also buy domain names that could be used to disparage the company, such as 'companynamesucks.com'. Control of a domain name will not stifle criticism of the company somewhere else, so it's better to focus energy on improving your business and website than trying to defend it against imaginary threats.

Buying your domain name

When shopping for your domain name, don't buy on price alone. If the company that registered your domain name folds, there is a risk that the name will get lost in an administrative limbo. Some companies register domain names cheaply as a loss-leader, knowing that they will recoup the money in hosting fees or transfer fees. Beware of any charges in the contract if you move the domain to a different hosting company.

External website designers will often register a domain name for you on request, and might charge an administration fee for this service. Be clear about what you get for your fee and consider whether you can bring any of the registration work in-house. You'll still need to have technical information about the website's servers which your design team will provide.

Like cars, domain names have to be 'parked' when they're not in use. If you don't have a server for your website yet, ask the company you buy your domain name from to park it for you.

Domain names are registered with administrative contacts, owners and technical contacts. Make sure that the domain ownership is attributed to your company correctly. It can prove difficult to get certificates for secure e-commerce if your business isn't the owner of your domain name.

Keep a record of when your domain names are due for renewal and make sure that payments are made promptly. If you don't renew your domain name, there is the risk that someone else (perhaps a competitor) will acquire it.

Make sure as well that you are getting your domain name registered and not just reserved. When new extensions are made available, many companies offer to reserve domain names using them. But this just means that they'll race to register your domain name when the extensions go live and there's no guarantee that other companies aren't accepting reservations on the same name or that you'll be successful in your application.

Redirection services

Redirection services enable your web visitors to type in one address and then be automatically taken to another address where your website lives. This can enable you to use free webspace and still get a proper domain name or a more memorable website address. But some redirection services require you to display adverts and others will charge you to use the service.

There's a big difference between redirecting your domain name and using a redirection service where you still don't get your own domain name. If you use a redirection service that doesn't give you your own domain name, you're still at the mercy of another company although your website address might be more memorable.

If you redirect your domain name, look for domain name 'masking', which is where your domain name appears to be the website address even when the visitor has moved to where your website really is. The problem is that any bookmarks will only ever go to the homepage and sites that want to link to you will either bypass your domain name to link to the real address of pages in your site or might be deterred from linking at all. The advantage of masking is that your real website address is hidden so that visitors will remember your address and not your service provider's.

Website redirection might be a good strategy for bringing supplementary domain names into your main website, but it isn't a good way to run the entire site.

Buying keywords

AOL and Realnames are two companies that will sell you keywords for use in their search engines. These keywords identify your company's website uniquely, like domain names do, and shouldn't be confused with renting a prominent position against search engine queries, which is discussed in Chapter 9.

The idea is that by using keywords people can type in your company name without any of the .com clutter and come to your website. If your preferred domain name is gone, the chances are you can still access the keyword and if your visitors are unfamiliar with the Internet, keywords can be shorter and less confusing.

But using keywords means tying yourself into specific portals for your traffic. You shouldn't stop promoting your domain name at all, so you will need to promote two different ways to reach your website. Having a website address and an AOL keyword could confuse your customers if they aren't comfortable with how the Internet works.

Consider how much of your potential audience has access to these facilities. Domain names are available on all browsers and all computers, but the availability of keywords will depend on what software people use or what service provider they subscribe to. In the US, it's often worth promoting an AOL keyword along with the website address because they can be much shorter and AOL has a significant market penetration there. Additionally, a lot of AOL users won't know how to use website addresses to access your site.

But if you do register keywords, be careful that your promotion doesn't confuse people about how they can reach your website.

Hosting checklist

For all but the biggest websites you'll want to deal with an external hosting company. They'll look after the server and make sure that your website is available over the Internet. Your designers just need to transfer the website and later modifications to the server electronically.

If you find that you need complete control of your hosting, you could set up your own server, but the staffing and cost implications make this unsuitable for small businesses.

The choice of a host is best left to your designers or someone with technical insight into how the website is designed. That said, you'll need to make sure that you know the answers to these questions.

- How many visitors can you have? Most hosts put limits on how much traffic you're allowed to have at your website, expressed as the amount of data downloaded in a month. Find out what happens if you exceed this. You don't want your website to be switched off because it becomes too popular for your pricing band. Check how easily you can upgrade, and how steeply the prices climb. Ask your website designers to express any traffic limits in terms of how many times your homepage can be seen in a month without breaking the rules. It's nothing better than an estimate, but it will indicate how many visitors you could serve at your homepage and show whether you've got enough capacity for the size of your customer base.

- How much space do you get? Speak to your designers to find out how much space they will need for all the files on your website. Chapter 5 reveals what makes a good website design. A well-designed site can go a long way towards cutting the amount of data that needs to be exchanged for each page view on your website, and therefore cutting both the amount of space you need and the traffic levels required.

- Can you get traffic analysis reports? You might have to pay more to get these, but as Chapter 11 shows, they can be a big help in assessing your website's success. Check whether you can have these added later and at what cost if you don't need them yet.

- How much does the hosting cost? What notice period is there for an increase in charges?

■ Is technical support available 24 hours? If you spot that the website's broken while you're at home, you'll want to phone up and have it fixed immediately. Companies playing to a global audience need to be particularly vigilant that the site stays open all hours. Find out how well staffed the support centre is.

■ Does the host forbid certain types of content? Hosts often ban political and religious views in addition to censoring sex and violence. Shops selling books, records, magazines or other information products will need to be particularly careful.

■ How often is your website backed up and how quickly can the hosting company restore websites from backups? Ask whether there are any guarantees of service levels. You might prefer to switch hosts than to try to enforce penalty clauses, but the targets still indicate the quality standards the host considers acceptable.

■ How fast is the server? One of the best ways to check this is to look at other sites on the host's servers, although how well the sites are designed can play a big part in that. Check in the morning, US time, which tends to be peak time on the Internet (although it will depend on the visitor demographics for the sites the server hosts). Make sure your technical team are confident that there's a good connection between servers and the Internet.

■ Can you conduct secure transactions through the server? If you plan to sell online or collect personal information, make sure that the server supports secure socket layer (SSL) security.

Summary

There isn't a good alternative to owning your own domain name. It's essential to your independence from your hosting company. Make sure that it's registered correctly in your name.

A domain name isn't worth anything until you start promoting it, so don't pay above the odds for a name.

Your website designers can look after the technology to make sure that your website's available, but you need to choose the domain name and make sure that the server and the hosting facilities will fit your business needs.

What makes a good website?

Anything that gets in the way of what customers need is
bad design, however nice it looks

Introduction

It's essential that your customers can use your site intuitively and can quickly find what they need on it. To manage your designers effectively you'll need to know enough about what makes a good website to be able to judge their suggestions and spot their mistakes.

The importance of good website design

Computer programmers and website designers love technology and enjoy discovering inventive new ways to use it. Channelled well, this trait helps your team to think creatively when making your website. But if you lose sight of why you're going online, you can end up with a beautiful but useless shell. Designers can get carried away with ideas that satisfy their creative need to build an impressive site but might not meet your business needs.

Picture the scene: you enter a high street shop in a hurry, knowing exactly what you need to buy. But before you can get past the door one of the cashiers insists on doing a dance for you. She's got rhythm, but you're not there for amateur dramatics. Given the choice between having to watch her perform or going next door to buy your goods, what are you more likely to do?

Many websites have animated title pages that do exactly this: they drive a wedge between visitors and the business and make it harder for customers to get what they need from the site. It's not difficult to see why this happens. Many managers in small businesses will judge websites by how impressive they look because they don't fully understand the business purpose of the site, how it will be used, or what the technology behind it does.

To help your business your website must serve customers. It doesn't matter whether you're selling them products, offering free software or just giving them information about your company. Anything that gets in the way of what customers need is bad design, however nice it looks.

Every click on your website is a decision point. Your visitors either decide to go further into your site or decide to go somewhere else or do something else. You won't always have their undivided attention and you certainly can't expect too much perseverance from them. If you bore them or make it too difficult to find what they want, they'll leave. They might even be viewing a competitor's website in another window at the same time as browsing yours. If you lose the customer, you might never have a chance to win them back again.

Good website designs get people where they want to be, quickly and happily.

©Nik Scott Illustrations, nikscott.com

The website design challenge

Brochure designers can ensure they don't have any words dangling untidily and can make sure that the readers can see all the important headlines at a glance on a page balanced with pictures and stories. Website designers can never exercise that level of control because they can't be sure what computer, screen size, font size or browser will be used to view the web page. Your visitors might be using a television remote control from across the lounge, might be sitting next to a computer with a keyboard, or might be using a Braille reader or a device that reads the website out loud to them.

The challenge is to create a website that looks reasonable on all screen sizes and all major computer and browser programs. Screen sizes vary so wildly that your site is likely to look spacey or cramped when varied from its ideal design size. As long as it works at the smallest size (640x480 pixels) and looks good at 800x600, your visitors have the option to reduce the size of their window on larger screens if it looks too much.

There's a compromise at play: the more sophisticated your website becomes, the more specific the visitor's computer setup will need to be to access it. If you have a website featuring just text and links, it will be accessible with nearly every device. If you have a site that has clever interactive animations, relies on identifying returning visitors or plays music, you narrow your audience to those with the right software and hardware installed for the site to work.

Sometimes you'll need to create several versions of the site to serve customers using wildly different hardware, such as mobile phones where there's a tiny screen and personal computers where there's much more space. If your audience matches the demographics for video games players, you might want to design a version of the site for best use with a game controller. If enough of your audience is using a particular technology, it's worth creating a specific version of the site to serve it. You can find out by asking your existing customers, or by following industry studies online or in magazines. If you have a high cost of customer acquisition and a high lifetime value of a customer, it's easier to justify the expense of designing several websites.

There's a weaker case for designing multiple versions of a website for different browser programs. The leading browsers upgrade regularly but stay backwards-compatible so that existing websites will still work with them. Sites using the new features of the browsers won't work with early versions though, and many people are happy to stay with an old version of the software because they are confident that it works and it's not worth the time taken to upgrade.

If your website designer suggests getting around the software compatibility problems by designing multiple versions of the website, don't let it increase the cost. Since you can't possibly imagine every incarnation of technology used to access the site (now and in the future), it's better to design a site that works well across as many different browser versions as possible than to create a site that pushes the boundaries of what's possible on each browser.

Using plug-ins to enhance your site

The standard browsers can be extended with programs called plug-ins that enable new types of information to be sent over the Internet. These plug-ins can usually be downloaded over the Internet for free. The manufacturers of the software make their money from the tools designers use to create the data and send it from the website. Example plug-ins cater for streaming video and audio (e.g. RealAudio) and 3D virtual reality environments (VRML).

Some plug-ins are widely used already (such as the Flash animation plug-in), so you are less likely to have any installation problems. The results of Flash can dazzle compared to plain text and graphics websites, but unless you need to use special effects for business reasons or to explain something more clearly, you should avoid them. Plug-ins tend to be slow to use and you're better off getting people straight to your business. Also, don't expect people to download a plug-in just for use on your site, unless that plug-in helps them to achieve what they came to the site to do. Even then the installation process is too intimidating for many Internet users.

Anything that might present compatibility problems should be a bonus for users with the right software, not an essential element of the site barring those without. If you want to use a plug-in or the advanced features of a browser, put the relevant pages in a separate section of the site so that users can choose to access them but aren't stopped from using your site if they don't have the right software. If you don't think people would follow a link to visit that content, it doesn't have any place on your website anyway. Give visitors installation instructions and a download link for any plug-ins you use.

Never allow great presentation to get in the way of a fast, effective website.

©Nik Scott Illustrations, nikscott.com

CASE STUDY

Virtual tours

Ski and snowboard holiday website www.iglu.com shows how plug-ins should be used. The site is using 3,000 iPIX® Virtual Tours to promote its holidays, but doesn't let them get in the way of using the website for bookings and gathering information on its products. The iPIX® plug-in lets visitors zoom into images and scroll 360 degrees around and up and down. Website users can stand in the middle of a hotel room and glance around it, or use another virtual tour to look around the town square. The tours are created using iPIX's patented process of taking two digital photos that face opposite directions using a fisheye lens. The iPIX software then meshes them into a single iPIX tour, ready for the plug-in. Iglu has used the plug-in to make the website a more entertaining and more informative experience than reading holiday brochures.

Customers shopping for holidays can use the iPIX plug-in at Iglu.com to zoom in and out of images and rotate the camera through 360 degrees up and down and sideways.

Image courtesy of Iglu.com and iPIX

Using pictures

Even as more and more people have fast Internet connections at their disposal, you must still use images (or 'graphics' in net-speak) carefully. They can make a website unusable until the images have downloaded. That can mean a long delay for those connecting over a telephone line which some visitors won't sit through. Many designers believe that all image constraints will be lifted by fast connections, but there are four counter-arguments.

■ Images will always compete with your text content. For every inch that's taken by an image, you're taking up screen space that could be displaying text that reinforces your corporate message. Your screen space is precious, especially the first glance before any scrolling. An ineffective image is worse than none at all.

- We're never going to see fast connections everywhere in the world. The lower the technology specification with which your website will work well, the larger your potential customer base.

- Some Internet-access technologies, such as Braille readers, voice browsers and handheld computers, don't support images as well as PCs do.

- Mobile Internet-access devices won't have access to fast connections a lot of the time.

It's true that a site without pictures can look boring and even unprofessional, and that a well-chosen picture can do the job of a lot of text. In the same way that broadsheet newspapers strive to have a picture above the fold so that they don't look dull on the newsstand, your website should aim to have a picture or several small pictures in the first screenful of the homepage.

But don't use graphics just to decorate your website. Use them to enhance its performance and your message. Photos of your team members or products can help to tell your story and showcase your corporate values. Stock photos of people staring into a monitor or laughing cheesily on the telephone – both website clichés that have spilled over from corporate brochures – don't help your site's effectiveness at all. Remember, people are waiting while they download this and some are paying in money (phone bills and Internet access charges) as well as time.

If you want to use pictures to break up a page or as visual cues to show people where they are in the site, make sure that the picture's relative unimportance is reflected by its rapid download time. If your website is supposed to sell things, don't display a beautiful but slowly unfolding shopping cart image. Don't delay those purchases.

Picture files are made of an arrangement of coloured dots (pixels), which can appear in any combination, including one that looks like text. Some website designers use this to get around the problem of not knowing what fonts the user has on their machine, but computers can't tell the difference between a picture of the president or an image of the words that make up his speech. That means the text won't index on search engines and can't be cut and pasted like normal text can, nor can it be searched with the browser's 'Find' option.

Text sent in a graphic file takes much longer to download than plain text. Restrict the use of this technique to where the appearance of text is business-critical, such as in your logo.

It's important to enforce a consistent visual identity across your website. With any click visitors could arrive at or leave your site, so you need to mark your territory clearly to avoid confusion. Use the same colours throughout and make sure that your graphics look as though they belong together, rather than being drawn from disparate library collections. Standardize on design elements where there's a choice so that all images have the same size border (or all don't have one), all headlines look the same, and spacing is the same between screen elements on different pages.

Your site's appearance needs to be a good fit with the target audience. It wouldn't look right to have cartoon characters lurking all over an industrial machinery retailer's website, but it would be ideal for a toy

Thumbnails give a small preview of an image which can then be clicked for viewing at full size. They stop visitors wasting time by downloading large images they don't need

Screenshot courtesy of Dan McDonald Photographic Design

shop. Likewise, a toy shop site that uses business-like but dull colours won't excite readers.

If you need to display large images, perhaps to show people the quality of a product in some detail, give people the choice of whether they want to see it or not. Use a small image (known as a thumbnail) to give visitors an idea of what the full image looks like and invite them to click to see it full size. That way you make the best use of limited screen space and don't clog up the connection with a slow image a visitor might not want to see.

Put your website address in the corner of photos your visitors might want to e-mail to friends so that anyone receiving the shot knows where it came from and might be tempted to visit your site.

Technology tips: images

This is the essential knowledge you need on how images work on web pages so that you can make sure your site is as fast and easy to use as possible.

- Make sure your website can be used with images switched off. You can easily test it by switching off images in your browser and then looking at the site, or asking your web designer to demonstrate. If there's nothing on screen, or you can't tell where the buttons are or what they do, it means that your site is useless until it's fully loaded or where graphics aren't available. That means it's much slower to use than it need be and can't be used at all by some web surfers.

- You should give graphics descriptive text (known as 'alt tags'). This text appears when the mouse rolls over an image in Netscape Navigator and Internet Explorer and is used in place of the image where graphics aren't available. The descriptions need to convey the same information as the picture. Don't just use descriptions such as 'picture' or 'button'; say something more revealing like 'company logo: link to homepage' or 'photo of our award-winning wedding bouquet'.

- If a web page tells the web browser how big the images are, it will set space aside on screen and then display the text straight away while the pictures download into their slots. Some website design packages (and designers) cut corners by not declaring the sizes and it can mean that nothing shows up until the final picture has started downloading. Make sure your web pages declare the size of all images.

- Personal computers keep recently accessed web pages and graphics files on the hard drive in case they're needed again. This 'cache' can be used to speed up your website if you use the same graphics across different web pages. The second time your navigation bar is needed, for example, it can be loaded quickly from the user's computer and won't need to be sent over the Internet again. Make sure your designers re-use images as much as possible. They'll need to have exactly the same filename and website address each time, not just look the same.

- Make sure your designers use the web-safe colour palette. Although personal computers can display millions of colours, there are only 216 colours that look the same across different computers and different browsers. If you don't use these colours, you run the risk of the site being unreadable on machines or with browsers you haven't tested.

- There's a trade-off between image quality and file size with the compression method used for photos (jpg). Low quality images look blotchy but download rapidly, while sharper images will take longer. Sometimes file sizes can be cut by as much as half with a minimal loss of quality. Get your web designers to find the optimum balance between download time and appearance. The size of graphics files (such as buttons, logos and line drawings) can be cut by reducing the number of colours in the palette. Remind your website designers to optimize the graphics for download time.

- You can often use coloured text boxes (known as tables) which download rapidly instead of graphics to split up a page.

Navigating your website

Your visitors must be able to find the information they need as quickly as possible. Although it is said that people should be able to find what they want in no more than three links, for most small business sites it should only take one or two.

Although you can put links anywhere, you need to have a consistent navigation panel (navbar) on every screen to help people get about the site. Make it easy to find by putting it across the top or near the top down a column on the left or the right. You should be able to see how to get from any section to any other section without having to go through the homepage or any other page that explains where everything is. You can have sub-sections by using menu screens, but you have to have everything linked into the main navbar somehow. This navbar should appear in the same place on every page.

Having the navbar on each screen is vital because you don't know which page people will arrive at. Some visitors will discover one of your pages through a search engine or link on another website and not see your homepage at first. Having your full navigation on every page gives them a flavour for what's on offer and also enables them to go anywhere on the site immediately.

People need to know what's behind each link as well. Don't use teaser labels like 'Have you seen..?' for promotional information instead of something clear like 'Seasonal discounts on gift wrapping'. You risk losing people who would have been interested because they didn't realize what a link was hiding. You want people to follow links because they want to read the content behind them, not because they're curious or puzzled.

On-screen links are eye-catching and voice browsers will summarize a page by just reading the text of links. Don't waste the reader's attention by having a link that says 'Click here' next to non-linking text that says 'For sales information'. Have a link that says 'Sales information' or 'Click here for sales information'.

To stop the navbar being unmanageably large, group items in a hierarchy. Don't list 120 products on the homepage, but divide them into categories (e.g. shoes, dresses, handbags). Once people have chosen their category you can go into more detail on the next page. If people had to scroll through 70 types of shoe and 120 dresses, the likelihood of them buying a bag from the bottom of the list would be slim. Use subheadings to make it easier to digest the menu at a glance: 'About our company' could subhead a box of links to contact information and the company mission; 'About our products' could title a menu of links to different product groups.

How you group items and how high up the list they come will depend on your site's goal. To generate maximum revenue from advertising, you need to get people to visit as many pages as possible, so you want to show the variety of content on the site to pull them in. If you're looking to get referrals from the site, electronic postcards or other referral mechanisms need priority. If you are aiming to sell from the site, reviews and product recommendations need to come first.

If your site has too much content to be fully listed on the navbar or the site hosts a product catalogue, add a search box so that people can find what they need by typing in a keyword. But make sure that you index the site properly so that it includes all the words people might want to use. The index should embrace your brand names, generic product types, business processes and names of team members known to the marketplace.

It's worth monitoring the keywords that people use regularly. If your visitors keep searching for the same thing, this should probably be more prominent in the navbar or should have a box devoted to it on the homepage (eg 'Looking for our new model cars? Click here'). If the same words keep coming up that aren't indexed, it suggests that either they need adding or for some reason you're attracting a lot of traffic that's mistaken about what your website does. Consider linking to another site that might be able to help them so you can cut down on e-mail inquiries.

Remember that any text or graphics on your website can link to other pages on the site. If you have a page that talks about the awards your products have won, you should link each product name to its page in the online catalogue. It's important to strike a balance here: you don't want to have a fog of every word being a link, but if it will help people to follow up ideas they're reading about, you should form links through the site apart from the navigation bar. Avoid using embedded links like this that leave your website – you'll keep visitors longer if you put external links in a dedicated section at the end of an article or on another page.

Using images in navigation

Your navigation bar is the most important part of your website: it's what helps people to find what they need. Don't let its appearance get in the way of its function.

If you can't tell by looking what a graphic button does, it's not doing its job. Buttons that only reveal their function when the mouse rolls over them, or (worse still) when they're clicked, make your site like a child's activity centre where visitors have to nudge buttons to see what reaction they get.

Make sure that any pictures you use on buttons or icons are clear to strangers when they visit. As images get squashed, it's easy to end up with something that you can identify only once you've seen the full-size version.

Good icons, such as an envelope for an e-mail link or a house for the homepage, can help people with learning difficulties to use your website and they also catch the eye easily when customers are looking for a link. Even though there are lots available, it's better to create your own so that you can make sure the images fit in with those on other navigation buttons.

Make sure that you design your navigation bar to be extensible. If you have to contrive a reason for putting content under a particular button, it's in the wrong section. If it doesn't seem to belong in any existing area of the site, you need the freedom to create one. You want regular visitors to become familiar with your navigation and don't want to have to redesign it every time you change the site content.

If you use graphics for your links, you need to include a full set of text-only links on the page too. Graphics can be slow to download and you don't want your presentation to get in the way of the site's function. Text links will load almost immediately, so people can start using the site before it's even finished loading. These text links are often placed at the foot of the screen. Remember that many people will switch off graphics to save time when they're in a hurry or looking at several websites in different windows.

So many sites put their logo in the top left-hand corner and make it a link to their homepage that it's almost a convention. It helps people to identify with the site and find their way home if they get lost or arrive at a page deep in the site and want to start exploring from the front.

Never have text that says 'Click on the image above to enter the shop' or something similar. If you're having to tell people where to click, your design doesn't work and you should change the explanation into the link itself ('Click here to enter the shop').

The role of the homepage

The homepage is your welcome mat. It's the first page people see when they type in your website address, though other visitors might arrive at different pages first, coming through links or search engines.

Don't waste time on the homepage telling visitors what you do. Start doing it.

examples

▶ The website replaces the printed brochure for a stationery company: the homepage shows selected offers from the catalogue and has a prominent search box labelled 'Search our catalogue of office stationery now'.

▶ A legal firm's website aims to build its reputation: the homepage includes news of recent changes in law, reports of recent court victories, and an editorial by the managing director about how the law is changing.

▶ A record label's website exists to make it easier to deliver products: the homepage shows what can be downloaded from the site straight away and offers free samples so that people can try the technology risk-free.

Although there's a tendency to try to impress on the homepage with lots of slow graphics, it's better to make the site quicker to get into and step up the time burden once visitors are already committed to viewing the content.

Every page on the site needs to link to the homepage. If people get lost or arrive in a distant backwater of the site, experienced surfers know the homepage is where you'll set them on the right path.

Meeting users' expectations

One reason the web is so popular on PCs is that it has a basic interface everyone can quickly learn. You click on links (they make your cursor into a hand) and you go backwards and forwards through pages using buttons on the browser. You fill in forms and click on buttons to submit them. You type in website addresses and can bookmark the ones you like to come back to later. It's that easy.

When people visit your website, they bring experience of how other websites work. Your site will be less frustrating and more popular if everything works in the way they expect it to.

One reason that animated websites can cause confusion is that they change the way links are used and screen displays are accessed. Persistent customers will spend some time working out what they're supposed to do. Most, however, will give up. If it's not obvious how your site works, you'll lose many of your visitors along the way.

Technology tips: Internet convention

As every good cook knows, sometimes the best ideas are not what to include but what to leave out. Here are the Internet conventions for accessing websites through computers that your designers might be tempted to tamper with. Don't let them.

- Text links are underlined. Don't confuse things by using underlining anywhere else. Use different colours or text styles for emphasis instead.

- The text links also have standard default colours, changing when a link has been visited. Choose a neutral, light background so that the links will show up with the default settings.

- The status bar at the bottom of the screen shows when web pages are loading and also shows where a link goes when people put the mouse over it. This helps visitors to see if a link goes off site or which part of your site it belongs to.

- The standard buttons used on forms for collecting information from visitors can look dull, but people are more likely to know how to use them than any fancy graphics you create.

Behind the scenes

So far we've focused on what the public sees of your website, but you need to also consider how it's put together behind the scenes and how the business is handled. There are plenty of off-the-shelf products for handling e-commerce and databases. These can be quick to deploy and are likely to be easier for another designer to find their way around than a stranger's bespoke programming if you have to change your web design company later. But be aware that the technology you use is likely to be obsolete in a couple of years.

If you have a large site with lots of text, your content should be stored independently of the design and be merged into web pages on demand when it's sent down the line. As new technologies are invented, it will enable you to draw on the same database of content and just create the new design instead of having to do everything from scratch. If your site is small, it's less expensive and less trouble to have a fairly basic website and create sites to serve upcoming technology as the audience for each new technology justifies it.

Testing the site design

You need to test the site to make sure that it's easy to use and it's compatible with the technology your customers will want to use in accessing the site. Make sure that you've tested the site on at least the leading software packages on the leading computers. A minor slip in the programming of a site might not matter on one machine (or bending the rules might even improve presentation), but it can stop pages looking good or even working at all on other computers.

It can be revealing to silently watch someone using your website, to see how long it takes them to find what they need. If they dither around looking for buttons or keep scrolling up and down the page, there's something wrong with the design. If you have a shop, you could put a computer in the corner and invite customers to try it there. You do not even need an Internet connection if your site can run off a disk or CD Rom. You can also ask people to test the site at home and let you know what they thought.

Give out feedback forms and invite ideas on how to improve the website. You can encourage people to participate by putting them into a prize draw. If you have forms for customers to complete on the site, try them out using the sorts of entries that customers might want to make in them. Make sure that you allow visitors to say the site works okay, so that you get a balanced view of how many visitors are affected by any problems. To check they visit the site, you could ask a question about one of the pages on it or could ask a few questions about the company. That will ascertain that they can find the information quickly, although it will motivate them to visit the sections with answers rather than the sections they would naturally be most interested in. Competitions are also a great way to build your mailing list database, but you'll need to comply with any relevant privacy laws (see Chapter 10).

Users who don't know your company to begin with will have different needs from your existing shoppers, so results from in-store tests won't represent your core audience if your website aims to attract new customers.

Don't forget you can put a survey on your website any time, although this solution is inherently flawed: if people can't get into the site to see the survey, they would be the visitors you would most need to hear from. See Chapter 11 for more information on assessing website performance, surveys, and how you can pick up clues for improving the website design using your traffic reports.

As well as testing that the design is intuitive, you'll need to test that the site works as intended. Your homepage button might work on one screen but not from another, for example, so the number of links to check can soon become dazzling. Fortunately there are websites to make your maintenance less onerous.

Netmechanic.com, for instance, will check the links, the programming, browser compatibility, load time and spelling on your website. In the same way that spell checkers are often foxed by proper nouns and words they don't know, no automated check of the design can be as foolproof as hand-checking everything, but Netmechanic.com is excellent at testing links and estimating download times.

Netmechanic will give your site a quick check-up, testing links and benchmarking download times and browser compatibility

Image ©Netmechanic Inc

Another helpful website is Bobby at www.cast.org/bobby. This checks for accessibility problems that might make your website difficult or impossible for the disabled to use.

Checklist: good website design

You need to be able to answer 'yes' to all of these questions. Refer to the main text in this chapter for more information on each.

- Is the site accessible for your customers, your future customers and your investors?

- Has the website been tested on different computers (at least Apple Mac and PC) with different browsers (at least Netscape Navigator and Internet Explorer) and different versions (at least the two most recent versions)?

- Can the site be used without any plug-ins?
- Are there explanations for content that doesn't work because the user doesn't have the relevant plug-in, together with a link to download it?
- Are the images functional rather than decorative?
- Has the site been tested with graphics switched off?
- Have you avoided text sent as graphics?
- Have the graphics been optimized for speed?
- Is the navigation clear and consistent?
- Can users see how to get to the homepage, whichever page they're on?
- Can users easily move between sections to find what they need without using trial and error?
- Does the homepage show why your site exists?
- Can people find out who you are and how to contact you quickly?
- Does the website use the default link colours?
- Does it have links underlined (and no other text underlined)?
- Does it leave the status bar clear?
- Does it use the standard buttons on forms?
- Does it pass the 'design crimes checklist' below?
- Has the site been tested by users?

Checklist: 16 crimes of web design

Amateur homepages make the web a richer place. They're bursting with ideas and enthusiasm and provided a training ground for many of today's most talented designers. But there are many clichés of amateur web design that make websites more difficult to use and make them look more like a hobby than a business. If your nephew is designing the website, or you're working with a fledgling design company, there's a risk that some of these elements of poor design will sneak into your site. Be vigilant for the following 16 design crimes.

1 **Animations**. Movement is distracting and wastes time. Abolish dancing envelopes and flying logos. Animations take longer to download than static images and if you're trying to keep visitors long enough to do business, time is money. (The exception to the animation rule might be advertisements, but see Chapter 6 for more about that.)

2 **Splash screens**. Any homepage that greets people and then tells them to 'click here to enter our site' should be binned. It's in the way. If the greeting has to appear, it can go on the homepage with the links to the meat of the site.

3 **Search engine trickery**. There are several techniques that can be used to try to fool search engines into giving your website a higher ranking. You can write keywords in tiny text which the search engine will pick up but which people can't read. You can create gateway pages crammed with keywords that exist just to get listed on search engines and bring people into the proper site. These techniques are often used by traffic-hungry amateur sites, but search engines threaten to ban any sites they find trying to cheat the system. It looks amateur and its dishonesty reflects badly on your business.

4 **Outlandish colours**. Unless you're in the children's entertainment business, you probably wouldn't meet a client in a pink suit and yellow shirt with flashing lights on your hat. It's not business-like. Make sure your website colours fit in with your company image and are easy to read. Most major websites use black text on white as the base colours and use contrasting colours for logos, navigation and highlighting.

5 **Frames**. Frames enable web pages to split the screen into windows, so that several different files can be on-screen at once. It's useful if you're integrating files from different servers, but if you own all the files, it does more harm than good. Content in frames can't be bookmarked and the site spacing can appear unpredictably on different browsers. Search engines can't index pages with frames properly either. Visitors sometimes arrive at one of your files without the rest of the site around it so they can only see part of a screen layout and can't get into the site. If your site uses frames, there should be an alternative non-frames version too.

6 **Counters**. Don't broadcast how many visitors your website has had, especially if it's low. You can get services (for free) that will display just a logo without revealing your level of traffic. See Chapter 11 for more on counters and other ways to assess your website's performance.

7 **Clichéd graphics**. This could never be an exhaustive list, but you can start by deleting:

- dancing envelopes and swirling @ signs for e-mail buttons;

- background images. These are repeated in the background of the page, but they either get covered by content boxes or make it more difficult to read the text. The most popular bad ideas are starscapes, virtual wood panelling, simulated exercise books and stone effects;

- bevelled buttons (especially if they're rectangular);

- graphics inspired by highway maintenance signs;

- graphic dividers that look like rulers, pencil-drawn lines, squiggles with cartoon characters at the end, 3D-effect horizontal bars;

- bobbles that come from the same collection as those dividers;

- free adverts for software used in making the site (e.g. 'Frontpage' logos);

- pictures with a corner curled over like a peeling photograph.

As the 'using pictures' section of this chapter reveals, images should never appear for purely cosmetic reasons and should have a job to do. It's important that the images all look like they belong to your website and not like they've just been lifted from a clipart collection.

8 **Deep pages**. Have one topic for each page and don't have pages that are several screens deep. Split longer content into manageable chunks and link them, unless it's important for people to be able to access a complete document (for example, a contract). Shorter content means it's all nearer your navigation bar so visitors have options within your site and they don't just leave it if they get bored.

9 **Centred text**. It's okay to centre headlines, but don't centre longer sections of text. Newspapers and magazines don't do it because it

looks ugly and it's more difficult to find the start of lines when reading.

10 **Unclear text**. Don't use ornate typefaces that look like they're handwritten or they're flowing from a pen in a gothic style. Use something that's easy to read at a glance. Your website won't lose any impact from people being able to read it clearly.

11 **'You are not worthy'**. 'I'm sorry,' some websites will say, 'your browser doesn't support this website. Please upgrade.' Ask yourself what is more likely: will people download and install new software to view your site, or they will go somewhere else instead? Design is about finding creative solutions and one of the problems of website design is that Internet users all have different computers and software. If the incompatibility warrants a warning, the site deserves a redesign.

12 **Scrolling text.** If a message is important, don't make visitors watch it crawl across the screen. Tell them in plain text they can read quickly. If it's not important, why's it there at all? The same applies to flashing text, which might draw the attention but isn't even on screen half the time.

13 **Status bar abuse**. The status bar at the bottom of the browser shows users when files are loading and the web address that links will go to as the mouse crosses over them. Some web designers think it's a good idea to scroll messages through this bar, or make descriptive text pop up in it when the mouse crosses a link. The status bar is tiny and many web users barely noticed it. If your visitors look there, it's because they want to see the default link address or download information. Anything else you want to say should appear in the main window. If it's not important enough to earn space on screen there, it's not important enough to put on the website.

14 **'Under construction' notices**. It shows poor planning and poor understanding of how websites work to say that part of the site is 'under construction' and not available. Websites evolve and few are ever 'finished'. Create a site that works fully, even if that's only one page, and expand it as new sections become available. Don't link to pages that aren't ready yet. That frustrates visitors.

15 **Poor layout**. You don't want to have huge spaces in your page, nor wide, uninterrupted tracts of text. You probably need a site that uses columns so that your text area isn't too wide and you can carry several messages in the first screenful. But don't run stories between the columns so that readers have to scroll up and down to read them.

16 **Music and sound effects**. It's so irritating to hear some cheesy tune play when visiting a website or hear whooshes as things move on screen. Music is disruptive (especially if it starts playing in a crowded office) and it slows the site down. Even the leading music websites are silent until you choose to play a song.

Summary

The website design is the packaging for the site's content and must help people to access it quickly. Part of the design challenge is making sites that work for different computers and browser programs, and you'll need to make sure that the site is tested on the most important ones.

Anything that might cause an accessibility problem needs to be an added extra on the site, and not central to its function.

You might need to steer your designers towards effective design for your business rather than impressive design, and you'll need to take special care with graphics.

You can use the checklists in this chapter to vet designs for any amateur clichés and make sure that the site follows the guidelines for good design.

Making money through advertising and affiliate programmes

This is the pocket money economy with payouts and business behaviour to match

Introduction

You can exploit the traffic at your website by selling advertising space. Although it can make a good contribution to the costs of running a site, carrying advertising is much less profitable than your core business should be, at least until you've got a substantial flow of traffic. And that means thousands of visitors a month, not the hundreds or even tens of customers that might keep a specialist business profitable.

This chapter discusses how much money you can make through advertising, the different options for selling advertising space, and how to make best use of affiliate programmes.

The myth of Internet advertising

Internet myth 'earn $$$ by linking to this site'

Everywhere you go online, you'll come across this promise. It's promoting an affiliate programme, where you're paid for visitors you refer to the site. But unless you're sending them a lot of traffic, you aren't going to make much money. (If you have got lots of visitors, see below for alternatives.)

This is the pocket money economy with payouts and business behaviour to match. You are competing with children who have set up websites about their favourite singers and teenagers putting their diaries online. They're happy to accept a few cents in advertising revenue and many affiliate programme operators aren't choosy about the quality of the sites they appear on. If they don't get any traffic, they don't pay any money anyway.

If you're referring visitors to a website, the prices are often quoted per clickthrough, which means you're paid for each time one of your visitors clicks the advert to go to the advertiser's site. Programmes pay about 10 cents per clickthrough at the high end, and rates of a couple of cents are common. At these rates, you won't make $$$ unless you're delivering a huge volume of traffic to their site.

The compensation poorly reflects the lifetime value of a customer referral. Next time a web surfer wants to go to the advertiser's site, they'll go straight there and you won't get any money at all. You're investing time in building loyalty to another company and almost certainly aren't getting paid enough for it.

Some programme operators have an excellent reputation, such as Amazon, which was one of the first. Others, however, think nothing of halving their rates at a day's notice or closing a programme altogether. Often you're left with nothing because there are minimum payout levels your account won't have reached.

Affiliate programmes imply that an advert is valuable only when somebody clicks on it and/or buys something. This isn't true. The links spread awareness of the brand name, even if they aren't followed up at that time. This is particularly the case with commission deals, where customers could nose around an affiliate operator's site for 20 minutes without earning you a cent. This visit is extremely valuable to the advertiser and it's not your fault if the site doesn't sell.

Get rich quick?

Work out the number of clickthroughs you'll have to deliver before you see any money. If a programme has a minimum payout level of US$25 and gives you $0.02 per click, you're going to have to send them 1,250 visitors before you see a cheque. Even if you had 10 per cent of your visitors clicking on the adverts (though 1 per cent is more realistic), you'd need to attract 12,500 visitors to your site before you would see a cheque.

And don't forget to deduct bank charges for converting currencies and cashing foreign cheques if you're not in the US. Most affiliate programmes are from the US and if you want to be a global player with your website, you'll have to lose your parochial attachment to your home currency and work with the best international sites.

Even when affiliate programmes become able to pay directly into online accounts and there aren't any cheque processing fees, the example above still illustrates the poor return you get for your work.

Affiliate programmes: what should you look out for?

Payment arrangement	Advantages	Disadvantages	Look out for
Pay per click: you're paid each time someone clicks on the link to the advertiser's website	Relatively easy for you to verify. You can design your website to count how often links are clicked	Low payout rates. Doesn't reflect the value of promoting the brand on your site	Intermediaries that offer consolidated cheques so you can pool the revenue from multiple advertisers to hit the payment minimum sooner
Pay per lead: you're paid when someone clicks on the link to the advertiser's website and then completes a form or joins a service	You can often get a signup form to go on your website, which increases the likelihood of signup	Difficult to verify. If you host signup forms, it blurs the lines between what visitors think is your site and what is the advertiser's	Payment rates nearer dollars than cents
Pay per impression: you're paid each time you display an advert to a visitor	You get paid when people just look at the adverts	Rare unless you've got extremely valuable visitor streams	
Commission on sales: you're paid a percentage of what customers spend after following your link to the advertiser's website	Much higher payouts when sales are made. Opportunity to recommend individual products and build a unique 'store' of links. Payment reflects the quality of the lead you send (you're rewarded if your referred visitors spend a lot)	Difficult to verify. Likely to occupy more screen space because you'll need to write persuasive copy and link to specific products. Doesn't reward you if a visitor goes to the site but doesn't buy anything. Income is staggered—you might display an advert without generating a sale for months and then refer someone who spends a lot of money	Programs that track customers and still pay you if they go away to think about it before buying

How to use affiliate programmes successfully

Ditch any dreams of affiliate programmes making you rich and they can become powerful tools for enhancing your website. They enable you to partner with other sites to offer new products and to broaden the range of customer needs you're able to fulfil. Your website is transformed from just promoting your business to being a one-stop shop for meeting all your customers' needs, making it more likely they'll come to you first next time.

examples

▶ If you run a childminding service, you could advertise educational toys, knowing that your clients have children and will respect your interest in their development.

▶ If you run a pet shop, why not link to books about caring for them, or nature videos?

There are other advantages to affiliate programmes:

■ If you want to link to the site anyway, you can often get a search box or signup form to go on your site by joining the affiliate programme. You'll make it easier for your customers to use the link, and you'll get paid if it's popular. The instructions make it easy to set up the links (about five minutes for the quickest).

■ You'll sometimes be able to co-brand the affiliate operator's site so that your name appears prominently on their site to visitors who follow your link. Sometimes there will be a link back to your website too.

■ If you want to carry advertising on your website, affiliate adverts can fill slots when you have spaces free. They can also be used to show potential advertisers where and how their adverts will appear.

If you review products from the standpoint of your customers, you can sometimes create a unique service. If you sell speech-writing services, review Winston Churchill's biography from the point of view of what made him such a respected orator. Use your articles to stimulate people to buy on impulse.

6 Making money through advertising and affiliate programmes

Here are some tips for making a success of affiliate programmes:

- Choose the affiliate programmes of websites that you might want to link to even if they weren't paying you. Don't link just for the cash.

- Look for a well-established programme that requires little maintenance once it's set up. Avoid seasonal graphics because they'll have to be changed.

- Avoid any programmes that advertise 'special rates' because they'll be cut back to the bone after you've signed up. Steer clear of programmes that say any important details – such as payment schedules, rates, payout levels – have yet to be finalized.

- Look for programmes that give you credit for the sale if the visitor goes away and then comes back to the site later to buy. People will rarely buy the moment they follow your link and will often think it over for a few days. Some programmes recognize this and flag visitors to your account for a month or more after you first referred them. This is more important for high-value products. You can expect to sell some books and cheap software on impulse, but you won't sell many cars in a single click. Not any decent ones, anyway.

- Don't link without trying the company first. Your reputation depends on their treatment of your referred customers.

- Interactive forms can be very effective in making the service appear integrated with your site and can help encourage participation. There might be a form for people to enter their e-mail address to receive a savings coupon, for example. Use text to make it clear that this is a special offer from another website so there's no confusion.

- Choose affiliate partners that you don't see linked to often. If you can introduce someone to a new website, you're more likely to get a clickthrough than if you link to a site everyone knows about anyway.

- Remember that reviews of any affiliate schemes online are usually on commission for referrals. While some reviews are incisive, many sites will make more from signing up other sites than from actually selling anything through the affiliate programmes.

- There are many intermediaries which will administer affiliate programmes for merchants. Some of these will consolidate the payouts from different merchants so that you get a single cheque and reach the payout level more quickly.

- Set the links to open a new window if possible so that your site stays on screen when your visitors follow a link.

- Don't do anything too contrived to accommodate an affiliate programme and be careful about the amount of time and energy they occupy. Remember that this is not your core business.

Working with advertising networks

With affiliate programmes, you take on the burden of arranging membership in the programmes and administering the links and graphics. Because they're open to all, they also pay poorly.

One alternative is to work with advertising networks, such as Valueclick and Doubleclick. They work as intermediaries, selling advertising space on your website. When you join the network, you include some code on your site that loads adverts from their server and they automatically change the adverts that your visitors see.

These intermediaries often send the adverts at random and some will even promise to do so, making sure that your core business isn't threatened by them deliberately selling competitors into the site. Sometimes advertising networks will categorize the sites in the network and offer advertisers exposure across all the sites in a particular segment. Doubleclick keeps track of other sites that visitors see and which adverts they click on to refine the relevance of adverts shown.

Rates are higher than with affiliate programmes, starting at 10 cents a click, but you'll need significant volumes of visitors before they'll take you seriously. Valueclick looks for a minimum of 15,000 adverts shown on your site a month and Doubleclick isn't interested unless you can offer a million.

There are some smaller networks asking for around 5,000 impressions a month, but you're still going to have to work hard to build that much traffic.

Selling your own advertising

By selling your own adverts you can subvert the game and break out of the 'quantity equals quality' mindset. Most online advertising at the moment uses a scatter-gun approach of flashing random adverts at visitors or, in the case of affiliate programmes, making the websites self-select which ads will be effective.

If you operate in a niche, though, you can charge advertisers a premium for the quality of your visitors and can charge them for visibility and branding on a strong site.

You might need to prove your visitor quality is good, of course. You can encourage visitors to register for site access and ask a few basic questions to assess their relevance to your intended advertising market. You might also need to prove that you've got the traffic levels you claim by getting your visitor logs audited (see Chapter 11 for more on assessing visitor levels).

But you'll be able to create flexible packages, selling a run-of-site package for a year so that an advert spends 12 months on all the site's pages, or offering them sponsorship of a section of the site.

If you embark on direct selling, you need a way to research potential advertisers and will need somebody to sell to them by phone or in person. You'll be competing for budgets with well-established magazines in most cases which are likely to have the first refusal on any website advertising.

The success of selling your own advertising depends on how uniquely you can profitably carve your niche, how well you can promote your website (see Chapter 9) and how well you can sell your advertising.

Are you introducing customers to your competitors?

Some of the websites you link to might later invade your business niche and rob you of custom from the visitors you sent them. The lines between information sites and retail sites are blurring. Publishers are marketing relevant products alongside their text and shops are using editorial to draw in visitors. You'll be best placed to judge whether sites you want to link to can overcome any entry costs to compete with you later.

But in one sense every advert you carry is for a competitor. The adverts will be designed to draw attention away from your main copy by flashing or by having screaming bright colours. If a visitor clicks on an advert, that's the end of their interaction with you unless they choose to come back.

©Nik Scott Illustrations, nikscott.com

Adverts are an invitation to leave the site, so don't include them on pages where you want the customer's undivided attention, such as the homepage and your shopping cart.

You could end up making less money the more adverts you display because the adverts also compete with each other. If you assume that a visitor leaving through a link doesn't come back, you'll lose the chance for them to click on other adverts. If each advertiser has a minimum payout level, you make it more difficult to reach any one payout threshold. Choose one company for each type of product and work with them. Don't promote competing sites.

An exception to this might be if your customers already have relationships with a store and the cost (in time or money) is high for them to switch. If you are a manufacturer promoting products that are available from multiple retailers, you could provide links to all of them so your visitors can buy from whichever is most convenient for them. There's a fine balance to strike between increasing sales and diluting where they go.

Make sure that the adverts are well designed or fix them so that they don't slow down the site (see Chapter 5 for tips on speedy graphics).

Keeping your site credible

Readers trust magazine and newspaper articles, so a glowing review of a product will have much more impact than an advert of the same size. That's why companies sometimes promote themselves with 'advertorials', or adverts that are designed to look like editorial written by independent journalists. These stories are sometimes headed 'advertising feature', but they still rely on the publishers renting out the credibility invested in their layout and editorial voice. Many magazine and newspaper publishers refuse to carry them.

In magazines it's relatively easy to spot the boundaries between advertising and editorial. On the web, it's not so easy. A site might be paid for every click on an inconspicuous link, and might therefore have a vested interest in getting you to click on it.

If you publish a glowing review for a product and follow it up with a link to buy it, you need to make it clear that you get a cut of the sales. If you don't, you can not only undermine that article but could also make readers suspicious of your motives in everything you say. They'll wonder whether your links and articles are for their benefit or whether you're being paid to include them on the site.

Defend your independence: don't be afraid to publish bad reviews if you don't like a product (but make it clear what you didn't like and still include the link to buy it). And don't endorse products or services that you haven't tested or can't wholeheartedly recommend.

On the web more than anywhere else, you need to win the trust of your visitors if they're going to become your customers. Don't blow it for a few dollars from an affiliate programme.

Some tips on keeping your site credible include the following.

- If the advertiser requires you to say the product is the best thing ever, don't carry that advert.

- Label adverts 'Advertisement'.

- Separate adverts from editorial by boxing them off or running them around the main copy.

- Consider putting your affiliate programmes into a section called 'store' so that people can see you're trying to sell things there and will know it houses promotional copy.

- Use the most popular advert sizes (see below), so people recognize that they're adverts on sight.

- Don't use anything that looks like an advert in your normal site design. Make sure that buttons and logos aren't the same size as standard adverts.

- Some adverts draw attention by looking like error messages or features of your website and these should be clearly labelled as adverts or avoided. Although sophisticated surfers realize they're adverts, newcomers can be alarmed and confused by them.

Standard advert sizes

There are several standard advert sizes. The most common is the 468×60 pixel horizontal strip, most commonly known as a 'banner ad'. This is usually placed at the top of the screen, with just enough room for your website logo to one side of it. Other common sizes include the 120×60, 120×90 and 125×125 boxes. Adverts sized 88×31 are used predominantly to promote website services. Experienced web surfers will recognize all these sizes as adverts.

6 Making money through advertising and affiliate programmes

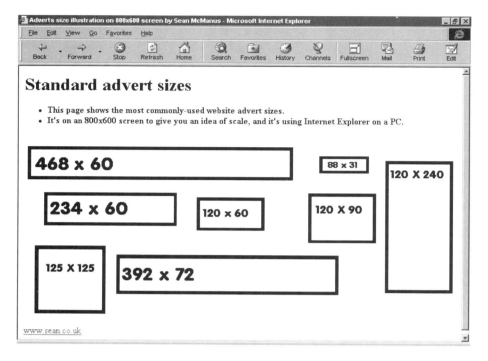

The most common standard advert sizes, shown on a webpage on an 800x600 screen to give an idea of scale. The measurements shown in the boxes are width by height, measured in pixels. Remember that your viewers might be using smaller or larger screens.

Investing in content and traffic

To sell advertising on the site, you've got to reach a strong target audience (either in quantity or quality) and you've got to keep visitors coming back. You'll need to have content that's updated often and although you can involve your visitors in creating that, it's going to need a big investment in personnel and technology from you first.

If you have a fresh idea for website content that nobody else can catch up on easily, you have the chance to become the web's dominant supplier in that niche. Most small businesses, though, will be more profitable diverting the investment that would be needed to make money from advertising into their existing business.

Summary

Membership of affiliate programmes can help to broaden your company's online offering, but it will make a contribution to costs rather than being a big money spinner.

Once your website reaches higher levels of traffic, you can join advertising networks that will sell adverts into the site automatically and will offer higher payouts for each click. Alternatively, you can sell your own advertising packages that reflect the value of branding directly.

You must remember that by putting adverts on your site, you're inviting competition into your business. Every advert vies for attention with your content and aims to divert readers out of your site and into the advertising site.

You need to make sure that the credibility of your website – and more importantly of your business – is not undermined by the adverts. Make it clear what you're being paid to say, so that visitors don't question your every word once they realize some text is sponsored.

It's going to take a significant commitment to building traffic and content to make money from advertising. If your lifetime value of a customer is high, your website could be profitable by delivering a few good leads a month into the business. To make money from advertising, however you'll need to promote the site ferociously so that you build a loyal and high-quality audience for advertising. Don't let this drain resources from your core business, which will be more profitable in most cases.

6 Making money through advertising and affiliate programmes

Selling from your website

Get customers to type in their order requests, their address and their credit card details and you have a sale

Introduction

Many companies can use their website to start distance selling for the first time, while others already selling by mail order can make it easier for customers to shop with them. There are no clumsy sheets of paper to fill in or envelopes to forget to post. Get customers to type in their order requests, their address and their credit card details and you have a sale.

Stimulating customers to buy

Some products lend themselves better to online marketing than others. The quality of tuna can be judged only by eating it, so customers aren't any better off reading the tin in a shop than they are on a website. But it is difficult to tell the colour and texture of clothes from a picture online, and you can't test drive a car with a mouse. Several companies claim to have invented products for sending smells over the Internet, but it will be some time before these are widely used, if ever.

For now customers have to depend mainly on your words and pictures when making their buying decision. All sites should show product packaging and many can help customers by including product reviews taken from magazines or written by customers. See Chapter 2 for more ideas for content you can use to promote your products and Chapter 10 for information on the copyright laws you'll have to comply with.

You can encourage customers to take a gamble on buying something by offering a guarantee that they can return anything they don't like in a saleable condition and you'll refund them. The business from wavering customers who commit to buy because of this guarantee is likely to outweigh the cost incurred handling returns. In some countries customers will have a legal right to return products they're not satisfied with. By publicizing the customers' rights, you can turn them into a promotional tool.

Make it as easy as possible for customers to shop at your website.

- Give them a virtual shopping basket, so they can buy several items in a single transaction.

- Give customers accounts so that they only have to enter their address and credit card details once.

- Help customers to shop by storing details such as their clothing size, or their usual shopping list.

- Let customers keep a record on their account of items they might want to buy later.

- Make it easy for customers to buy presents by sending their gifts to the recipient. Offer a wrapping service and let customers personalize a note you enclose. You can even keep track of their friends' birthdays and suggest suitable presents. If customers can't work out what to buy as a present, offer them a gift voucher.

- Tell customers how much postage and packing will cost up front so they don't have to hunt through the site to find out.

- Give customers a phone number they can call so you can help them use the site or can take the order by phone.

Selling information products

In some cases, you can charge readers to access your website, but you'll need to offer something exclusive. Niche publishing that could not bear the costs of printing and distribution is viable because of the Internet, but mass market information is free now that newspapers and magazines upload their entire content for nothing.

One problem with selling website content is that you can't easily charge customers small amounts. Ideally, readers would be able to mix publication sources online and buy their news from one newspaper, their book reviews from their favourite magazine and not bother with all the lifestyle pages that are binned unread each Sunday. But credit card charges and customer concerns about security make small payments unworkable for small value transactions. Even when suitable payment mechanisms emerge, you'll need to keep bringing customers back to create a reasonable income stream. A better business model is to charge a subscription fee for unlimited access for a certain time period.

You might also be able to sell one-off file downloads, which could contain songs, words, pictures or anything else that can be put on a computer. You can increase the perceived value of these digital files by designing pretend packaging for them. If you're selling a 120–page market report, design a cover so it looks like a book on the website and tell people they can download it instantly. If you're selling music downloads, show them CD cover artwork and explain that they can get the 12 songs in minutes by shopping online and downloading them.

If your content requires any special software to make it work, give customers full information on how to use it and provide links so they can download it. You might persuade customers to download the popular plug-in Adobe Acrobat to read your electronic book, but if you don't tell them how to do so you'll instantly restrict your market to those who already have it installed. Let customers test the system by offering free sample files so they know they won't get caught buying a file they can't open.

The best promotional tool you have for an information product is the product itself – you can offer a free trial access to your website, or offer extracts of a market report you're selling. It doesn't cost you anything to reproduce as many free samples as people want.

Piracy can be difficult to prevent with digital products. How do you stop customers from sharing website passwords? What happens if they copy your downloads for friends? There are software solutions to stop files from being copied, but you'll have to compare the cost of them with the likely hit on profitability if you don't use them. It might be more profitable to trust customers unless selling information is at the heart of your business plan.

There's a trade-off as well between security and convenience. The more secure you make your files, the more inconvenient they are likely to be for customers to use legitimately.

Accepting payment

Shops and other businesses that accept credit cards have a 'merchant account' for processing those orders. However you don't have to have your own merchant account to accept credit card orders if you partner with other websites that process the transactions for you.

There are several ways that you can accept credit card payments from visitors to your website:

- You set up (or already have) your own merchant account. You collect credit card details through your website, and you then authorize these in the same way you authorize your shop transactions, by phone or using a tabletop machine.

- You set up your own merchant account and partner with a company that will supply software to authorize transactions as they happen in real time. This is essential if you're selling downloadable files because you need to authorize the transaction before you give the customer the product.

- You pass all your shopping transactions through a website that accepts credit cards on your behalf. These services can be a good way to trade if you're just selling a few products but don't always provide the shopping cart and advanced features necessary to operate a full shopping site. Because the credit cards are accepted on a different website, you need to take care that the customer isn't confused. You also need to be aware that you don't own your shopping page if it's hosted on another website. If your company name won't appear on the customer's credit card bill, remind them whose name will so that they don't complain the transaction is fraudulent when they see it on their statement. Sites that will partner with you like this include www.ccnow.com.

- You use a virtual account service, such as www.paypal.com. This acts as a virtual bank account, enabling anyone to send money to anyone else over the Internet. Credit cards are used to deposit and withdraw cash.

This area of Internet business is changing rapidly and small businesses are well advised to speak to their banks to see what services they can offer. If your site is just selling a few products at low volume, it can be cost effective pushing those orders through another site or at least testing the market that way first.

But to create a more professional impression, businesses should set up their own merchant accounts and accept credit cards at their own website. If you accept personal information or credit card details at your website, you'll need to have a secure server.

Securing your server to accept credit cards

To secure your server, you need to get a server ID (also known as a digital certificate) from a certification authority such as Verisign (www.verisign.com). The system works because customers know they can trust the certification authority, which goes to great lengths to make sure that websites are legitimate businesses before issuing certificates. When pages are secured with a certificate, the browser will show a locked padlock icon.

Secure certificates enable all communication between the user and the server to be encrypted so that only your server can understand it. Even if data goes astray, it will be meaningless and impenetrable to anyone else who finds it. A secure connection will also add a code to messages that will show if they are tampered with or corrupted in transit.

Most servers now are compatible with secure IDs, but make sure you ask your designers to check for this when finding somewhere to host your website.

Few companies deal directly with the certification authority, delegating this job to the website design team.

Reassuring the customer

Many customers believe that electronic commerce is risky. They are afraid that their credit card details will be stolen on their way to the trader, or that the trader might just be a front for a credit card scam that's collecting numbers to rip off.

These are valid concerns, but e-commerce is no riskier than how credit cards were used before the Internet. When orders are placed by telephone, anyone could be listening in on a crossed line and when waiters disappear to process a credit card, they could easily take a copy of the card for their own use.

To overcome customers' concerns, explain how the technology works. Your secure ID will be effective only if customers trust it and understand what it means. Tell visitors that if their browser shows a locked padlock icon, their information is encrypted so nobody else can understand it but you. Tell them about the background checks that your certification authority made before granting you your server ID, and link to its website to provide more information.

Customers will have more faith if they know that their credit card won't be debited until after the goods are sent. For some products you can include an option to bill customers later, so that they can pay by cheque after they've approved their purchase.

More sales by integrating the website with the business

A recurring theme of this book is how you can integrate your website with your existing business, and your sales routine is no exception. Customers often visit shops to browse and think it over before deciding what to buy. When they've made up their mind, your shop might be closed but the website's still open. Send customers away with information on your website if they're not ready to buy in the shop so that they know they can order online if they want to.

You can also use the website to bring customers into your premises. Perhaps your customers could book appointments on the website and then come in for a personal consultation, or they could reserve a product for collection in the shop. If your sales team is well briefed about what is on the website, and the customer is told who on the team specializes in what they need, your business will be in a stronger position to continue the dialogue the website began when the customer arrives. Provide customers with directions to your business on your website and include transport information.

Don't forget that making help available in your shop or on the phone can increase the customer's confidence in website sales. Customers want to be able to walk into your shop with the product if they can't get it to work or they want to return it. Don't make them return goods by post just because that's how they received them.

CASE STUDIES

Real world meets cyberspace

Here are three case studies that show how websites are being integrated with real-world businesses to make it easier for customers to buy.

Argos operates a chain of catalogue shops in the UK, where shoppers visit a store and choose goods from a catalogue which are picked from the warehouse on site for immediate collection. The website at www.argos.co.uk has a Click and Collect service that lets people reserve products online before travelling to their nearest store to pay for them and collect them.

Cinemark Theaters sells tickets for cinema screenings across North America from its website in partnership with Fandango (www.fandango.com). Customers can buy their tickets online and print them at home. A similar idea has been used by European airline Buzz which has dispensed with tickets. Customers just bring the booking number the website gives them, although they can print the reservation information for reassurance. When issuing tickets online, barcodes and booking numbers can be used to ensure that there is only one admission per ticket.

Netpack (www.netpackage.com) sells subscriptions to news websites through retail stores. Customers buy a packet and pay for it at the till. The packet contains a password giving them access to the website. The payment model is similar to that used for some mobile telephone subscriptions.

Summary

Your website can make it easier for customers to shop with you, as long as it's planned with care. Include shopping baskets, accounts, gift recommendations and any other features that will save customers time.

Not all products are a good match for online sales, but you can encourage customers to take a risk by offering a guarantee that they can return products they don't like. Digital products such as electronic books, song files and games are good for online selling because they can be easily distributed, but you might need to invest heavily in anti-piracy measures if this is central to your business plan.

There are several different ways you can accept credit cards for payment, even if you don't have your own merchant account. Any websites you partner with should be easy for customers to use and offer a smooth transition between your site and theirs.

If you are accepting credit cards at your website, you need to invest in a secure server ID. To make best use of it, explain to your customers what it means so that they can overcome any doubts they may have about trading with you.

Make the website one of your sales channels that serves your customers and don't treat it as an isolated business. If you can use your walk-in business to take people to the website, or can use the website to bring people into your shop, you'll give them a choice about how they want to shop from you and will be able to offer greater flexibility and a better level of service.

7 Selling from your website

Offering great customer service online

Seize every opportunity to open correspondence with site visitors so you can help them to win confidence in your business and encourage them to become your customers

Introduction

If you are using your website to attract new customers, their first impression of your business will come from what they see on the site and how you handle their e-mail. This will help them judge your reliability and trustworthiness.

If you're hoping to migrate existing customers to the web (to save costs, increase how much customers buy, or make them return more often) you'll fail if you can't help those people as much as you do on the phone or on your premises.

Whatever your website purpose, you must ensure that e-mail replies to customers are accurate and prompt.

Training the team

Make sure that anyone responding to customers can spell correctly and write clearly and that they check e-mails before sending them. Many companies have sacrificed accuracy in the shift to e-mail and messages are sent with typing errors that would never be allowed in a printed letter. It creates an impression of hurry or carelessness, both of which seem dismissive towards customers.

While you might have recruited your existing customer service team for their talent on the shop floor or telephone, they'll need different skills to offer great service by e-mail. Apart from training the team to use the software and hardware required, you should consider offering guidance on spelling and punctuation and how to structure e-mails.

Encouraging customers to get in touch

Whatever your website does, your business will almost certainly need to have some 'real-world' contact with your customers, whether that's by shipping products, arranging meetings or just taking phone calls. When dealing with websites, customers are asked to make a leap of faith. Based on a few screenfuls of information, they're asked to trust you to deliver the goods or to be on the phone when they need you. Sometimes they're asked for personal information, including credit card details.

So you should seize every opportunity to open correspondence with site visitors so you can help them to win confidence in your business and encourage them to become your customers.

You can increase incoming e-mail by making it clear you want to hear from visitors. Offer to help if they can't find what they want on the site. Invite them to contact you for a price quote for their job. Ask them to tell you what they think of the website and include contact information prominently on every page.

You can make the site friendlier by including the names of key team members. If you tell customers that Jim, the customer service manager, is looking forward to their e-mails they'll be able to e-mail him personally. The type of letter sent to an anonymous 'Sir/Madam' in a customer service department would be less relaxed and less revealing than a letter addressed to 'Jim'. If customers aren't comfortable with e-mailing companies they don't know, having a name helps to break down barriers.

Quality callback

How easy can you make it for customers to contact you? Prime Hospitality Corp in the US has a callback service on the websites of its Amerisuites and Wellesley Inn hotel chains (at www.amerisuites.com and www.wellesleyinnandsuites.com). The system, supplied by Communication Enabling Technologies (www.4cet.com) enables website visitors to complete a form on the site with their phone number and e-mail address so that a customer service representative phones them straight away or after a customer-specified delay. Customers who aren't comfortable booking online, or who have questions which aren't answered on the site, have the option of speaking to someone straight away.

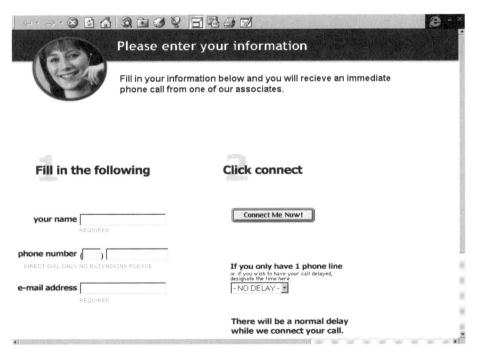

Websites that use Communication Enabling Technologies' system can offer to phone customers while they're still on the website

Image courtesy of Communication Enabling Technologies, www.4cet.com

Include a phone number and a postal address on the site as well (not just a PO box). This reassures customers that your business is legitimate and many still prefer to use the phone as their first point of inquiry.

A quick and clear reply to an e-mail enquiry can boost confidence in your business, but failure to reply can have the opposite effect. Make sure that you have a system for fielding incoming e-mails so they are sent to somebody who can help and they're answered as quickly as possible.

Using feedback forms

One popular way to smooth the flow of inquiries is to make visitors complete a form on the website to contact you. The form can guide them into providing all the information you need, and it enables those without their own e-mail addresses to send messages through the website. You can ask visitors to select which department they want to contact and have their correspondence automatically forwarded to the right person, and can also make them pre-select the type of message they're sending. E-mails about product failures could then be easily prioritized over brochure requests.

CASE STUDY

The right image

Customers struggling with Roland DGA's imaging products can turn to the website for technical support. The RxPress site at www.rolanddga.com/support gives customers a form to send their questions to the 11-person technical support team. Most questions are answered in 20 minutes by e-mail with step-by-step instructions. In its first month the site received more than 1,000 inquiries. The website also publishes a library of frequently asked questions and product manuals and the company continues to offer telephone support. E-mail forms like Roland's that help to clarify the query and then divert it to the right person can help to speed up response times.

Forms should be used where they can make communication easier and not just to replace e-mail addresses, which are more convenient for customers. When customers e-mail you their software keeps a copy of the message for their records and they can use the whole screen to compile their message and can edit it with ease. While an e-mail address can appear on every page of your site, customers will have to go to a separate page to complete an inquiry form.

Long forms are intimidating, especially if they demand personal information visitors don't want to share yet and the forms won't accept any inquiries without being fully completed. It's awkward to enter a message in a tiny scrolling window, and it's absurd that some forms limit the amount that customers can say. It will take them longer to type than it will take you to read. Customers must feel strongly about your business to want to write at any length and these are the people you most need to hear from. Make sure that your forms don't deter customer contact.

example

► If the shopping facility on your site stops working, you'll find some visitors will happily take a minute to e-mail you to tell you so you can fix it. With subtle design problems, only a fraction of visitors will be affected and you won't know unless they tell you. If the only way they can get in touch is by completing their name, address, e-mail, phone number, fax number, operating system, browser version and finally message, they won't bother. They don't need to do you a favour that badly.

If you want to use a feedback form, give people the choice about which boxes they complete and give them an e-mail address they can use instead. It's better to have business leads you can pursue for incomplete information than to have no leads.

Increasing confidence through security

It's obvious that credit card transactions need security because of the risk of fraud, but what about personal information? Wouldn't customers be more comfortable completing forms and e-mailing their data if they knew it was secure? Browsers are often set by default to warn their users if any information is being sent over through an insecure form. Warnings like that can scare customers away. See Chapter 7 for more on website security, and make sure you extend it beyond financial transactions to anything customers might want to protect.

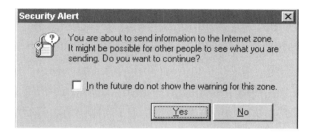

Security warnings like this one from Internet Explorer can deter customers from sending you information through your website forms

Screenshot reprinted by permission from Microsoft Corporation

There are encryption systems that will scramble e-mails so that they can be decoded only by the intended recipient. E-mails are encrypted using one password, and decrypted using another. The passwords are related, but the mathematics involved makes it impractically complicated to work out the access password from the locking password. You can freely publish the password to lock files (the 'public key') on your website as long as you keep the unlocking password (the 'private key') secret. That way customers will be able to send you e-mail messages that they know only you can decode, even if someone else intercepts them. The best known program for this type of public key encryption is PGP (which is short for 'pretty good privacy').

Customers expect the best

Businesses no longer just compete with companies in their own sector; the service customers receive is compared between companies in different industries. And while a few weeks might be acceptable in replying to a letter, e-mails demand faster turnarounds. They take seconds to write, and customers expect a prompt reply.

example

▶ Imagine an online business that sells industrial machinery that costs as much as a house. A businessman finds the site and excitedly e-mails an inquiry about availability, then goes to an online bookshop to buy a present for his wife. The book's out of stock, so the customer e-mails the shop asking when it might become available again. The next day one e-mail arrives. It's from the bookshop with expected reprint dates. Nothing arrives from the industrial supplier for several days.

It might seem unreasonable to busy managers in small businesses, but customers will wonder why one company can make time to tell them about a $10 book when another takes days to help them with a major contract. Customers will wonder: 'If they're not even that eager to help me buy it, how quickly will they respond if it breaks down?'

Use autoresponders to reply immediately

Luckily software can reply immediately on your behalf. Autoresponders are programs that will send a standardized response as soon as an e-mail is received. You can use this to reassure customers that you're looking into their inquiry, tell them what the typical response time is and inform them if there might be easier ways for them to get the information they need. Make sure that you follow up on the promise and respond, though.

Don't let your administration in the business bring inquiries to a halt when they reach you. Divert e-mails quickly to the right person and set target times for a response. You can make it easier to sort incoming e-mails if the e-mail links on your website automatically set the e-mail's subject when they're clicked. That way you'll have subjects such as 'e–mail from homepage' or 'shopping cart inquiry' instead of subjects like '<no subject>' and 'question' which will force you to open the message before you can decide who needs to respond to it.

> **Date:** Thu, 18 Jan 2001 10:39:43 +1100
> **To:** [customer's e-mail address]
> **From:** [your e-mail address]
> **Subject:** Thank you for your inquiry
>
> Many thanks for your inquiry. One of our customer service managers will contact you soon. If your inquiry is urgent, please remember you can call us on +1 555 5555.
>
> You might also find it helpful to read our list of frequently asked questions on our website at www.examplewebsite.com/faq.htm
>
> We look forward to working with you!
>
> Jake Sinclair
> Managing Director
> Example Company

Example autoresponder e-mail

Easy e-mails that show you care

You can make it easier to respond consistently by using standard e-mails that are hand-tailored to inquiries. Including the sender's name and a couple of references to their inquiry is all it takes to create the impression of a personal service. You might, for example, have an 'out of stock' message into which you can insert the product name and expected due date.

The personalization is important. Sending another copy of the brochure when that's what prompted the query sends a clear message that you're not listening. If you think you have a standard e-mail you can send without any customization, you should ask why the information isn't on your website or why customers can't find it there.

If customers send questions that are already answered on the website, it's still better to e-mail the information than refer them to the website. If you do have to direct them to the website, tell them exactly which page the answer is on, and give them a link to go straight there. Invite them to e-mail again if after reading it they have further questions and tell them you'll be pleased to help. It's tempting to think these people are stupid because they haven't looked at the site properly, but they're helping you to refine your design. Their inability to find what they need is down to your failure in designing the website navigation as much as it is down to their inability to use it, so consider how the site could be improved if a pattern in puzzled e-mails emerges.

Don't scramble your message

Computers enable us to format our letters in a way we never could before. We can align text automatically, change its size and typeface, give it colours and insert pictures and logos. We've come a long way since the typewriter.

By comparison, standard e-mails can look naked. They're just text and space. Raw information.

The temptation is to start jazzing them up with colours, fonts and pictures, and some e-mail programs will support this. But unless you're confident that the recipient has an e-mail program that can understand this finery, you risk your message getting lost in a soup of computer code. The presentation should help to enhance your message, but for people with incompatible software the message can get lost. Some people switch off the advanced formatting features because viruses can exploit them to infiltrate the computer.

Another way to control the presentation is to send a well-designed document from your word processor. Attachments are files, such as documents, spreadsheets or even games, that are sent with an e-mail message. They're often marked with a paperclip icon by the e-mail program. Now your readers have to open your e-mail, then open the attachment before they can see your message. And they still need compatible software to be able to read it. Attachments can spread viruses and take longer to download than plain text messages, so they should be used only when you're sending the file itself to someone for them to use, rather than using it to carry information that could go in the e-mail. Don't let your e-mail program automatically send an attachment, such as another version of the message or an electronic business card. Some do this by default.

To ensure that people can quickly read your message without any technical barriers, just send plain e-mails. You can use subheadings in capitals, and use characters such as dashes to separate sections. Plain text e-mails will help you to concentrate on the message and not how it looks, will be quicker to write and download, and will be universally readable.

Defending your business against viruses

Viruses are programs that exploit weaknesses in software such as e-mail and word-processing packages to send instructions to take over a computer. They're able to spread themselves by e-mailing themselves to you from an infected machine or adding themselves to every file created. They can delete files and break programs or just make machines misbehave slightly. The person who infects you won't know they're a carrier, and won't know the virus has been sent. It's extremely rare for someone to deliberately send you a virus.

There are several precautions you can take:

- Install anti-virus software. New viruses emerge all the time, so software should be updated as often as possible. Think of update periods of days or weeks here, not months.

- Don't accept unexpected e-mail attachments. Jokes and games that are sent by e-mail might play well, while mangling the hard disk in the background. Even documents could include a virus that the sender doesn't know about, so ask for a plain e-mail if possible and virus-scan any legitimate files before opening them.

- Beware of any out-of-character e-mails. If your friend's computer had a virus, it might look up your address in the address book and automatically send itself to you. If you get an e-mail from a business associate with the subject 'Joke', and you don't usually share jokes, check with him before opening it. The machine might have sent it automatically, and in that case it won't be funny.

- Make sure that your data is reliably and regularly backed up. If the computers are destroyed, you could rent new computers and copy the data on to them to keep the business running until a more permanent solution can be found.

- Isolate important machines. Don't connect the accounts machine to the office network or the Internet, for example, and restrict the passwords to those who must use it. Set it up to check all disks automatically for viruses.

Handling hoax viruses, jokes and junk e-mail

When there's a virus outbreak, people warn their friends. Those people then forward the alert to their friends and before long, everybody knows about it. Most of the warnings that you'll receive are hoaxes though. The warnings are started as a joke or to see how far they'll go and they spread fear and uncertainty. The e-mails also undermine the impact of genuine virus warnings and clog up the Internet, increasing the costs that service providers must pass on to their customers.

Hoax virus warnings aren't that difficult to spot. They'll usually follow this pattern.

- They threaten dire consequences, such as hard disks being erased, computers being broken. Some real viruses can do this, but most viruses have a relatively benign payload. You don't see hoax warnings threatening moderate danger.

- They claim that the warning was issued by a major computer company, software house or news organization. But they don't justify this claim with a link to the appropriate website, and it won't be found on the sites of those companies if you check.

- They tell you to 'forward this message to everyone you know!!!!!'

- They have bad grammar and use dramatic language.

If you receive a virus warning, check whether it's genuine or not by visiting one of the leading virus hoax websites (such as www.vmyths.com) or searching the web. If it is fake, it's best to reply to the sender and tell them it's a hoax, tactfully thanking them for warning you about what they thought was a genuine risk.

Even if the virus risk is genuine, the warning is rarely worth forwarding. So many viruses run wild now that unless there is a threat from something new and you recommend action people can take to protect

Visit www.vmyths.com to verify virus warnings. This hoax-busting site is run independently of any software companies

Screenshot courtesy of Vmyths.com

themselves, it's not worth spreading alarm. If you do forward a virus warning, include a website address at a reputed anti-virus company so that the message carries credibility and isn't dismissed as a hoax.

E-mails that are junk to you might be sent in good faith, such as virus warnings. Jokes are another example. The same 50 or so humorous e-mails do the rounds, becoming less funny each time and draining resources. Ask contacts to remove you from any joke distribution lists if they add you without asking.

If your business (or anyone in it) sends out joke or scare e-mails, it will undermine the impact of any future messages you send. If you send too much junk, people will add your e-mail address to their filters so that your messages go straight to the bin without them even having to know. Even if they don't do that, they will at least give your e-mail less avid attention than other incoming messages.

8 Offering great customer service online

137

Once your e-mail address appears on a website, it's easy prey for spam robots which crawl the web looking for more people to send junk e-mail to. Some messages will say 'ADV' in the subject line to tell you it's an advert, while others will be impersonal sales pitches. Many will be about get-rich-quick schemes or pornography. The messages often feign ethical behaviour by offering removal instructions if you don't want to get more junk e-mail. Following these just confirms that your e-mail address works and so leads to more spam being sent. If the spammers had any sense of ethics, they wouldn't be sending junk e-mails at all.

You can minimize your spam by using fewer e-mail addresses on your website, but you need to make it clear to your team that they should simply delete any junk e-mail.

Your team and personal e-mail

Your team members might want to use e-mail to keep in touch with friends and family or to use the Internet to research their own interests. Unions have objected to companies that spy on employees' personal activities or forbid them, and companies have replied by pointing out that they're paying for the technology and the time.

Businesses benefit from a team that uses the Internet frequently. More experience online can only lead to new ideas from other websites being brought into the company (assuming there's a suggestion scheme). Likewise, companies that refuse employees any personal phone calls and personal e-mails don't create a cooperative environment. The team won't stay late if there's a business emergency. Staff turnover will be higher.

There can be problems, though. Unmotivated employees or those without self-discipline can allow their surfing to consume work time. The problems here aren't with the introduction of the Internet as much as with how the employee fits in with the business.

Another problem is that it can reflect badly on the company when jokes, political chain letters and hoax virus warnings are forwarded from the company's e-mail addresses. Some companies add an automatic disclaimer to all outgoing e-mail, saying that it doesn't necessarily reflect the company's views, but you might want to allow personal e-mails to friends and relatives, and forbid impersonal circulars.

All businesses should have an e-mail policy so that employees know what is expected of them.

Offering live customer service

With e-mail there's a time lag in replying. It's faster than exchanging letters, but there's still a delay until the recipient opens it and reads it. It is possible to offer help to site visitors while they're on the site using a chat program. Visitors can put their questions straight away to a real person, who replies as soon as they're received. Your team can guide visitors on how to make the most of the website and personalized selling becomes possible. If the customer service team is away, visitors can leave messages.

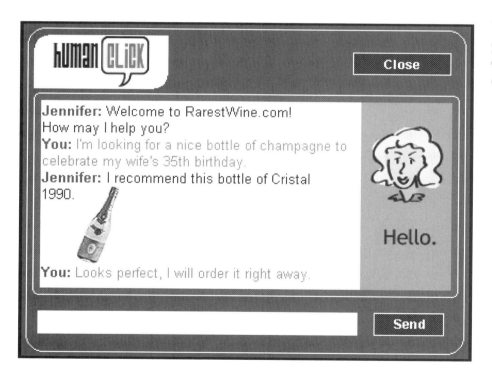

Website visitors can request immediate help from customer service representatives using Humanclick

Image courtesy of Humanclick.com

Any business that has a permanent Internet connection or has members who need to spend a lot of time online can use chat to engage customers passing through the website. There are standard chat programs that are integrated with browsers, such as Netscape's Instant Messenger, and there are popular free standalone programs such as ICQ (www.icq.com).

Humanclick (www.humanclick.com) provides a dedicated customer service chat application. Visitors click on an icon to indicate they want to chat, and a window opens with a space for visitors to enter their text and a window that shows the full conversation, both the company's side and the customer's. Operators can conduct three simultaneous chats and can draw upon standard responses to help speed up replies.

Integrating the website with the company

Your website must be integrated with your whole company to ensure that customer service is consistent. Anyone answering the telephone needs to be able to help customers who struggle with the website. If they can't answer technical questions themselves, they need to know who to transfer the call to.

Everyone on the team needs to know the website address and what's on the site so that they can recommend it when it's the best way to help customers. If you have website designers fielding e-mails, they need to know how to get customer questions to the right people in the business quickly.

You also need to be clear if there are limits to which questions each team member should answer. If you're selling advertising on the site directly, you'll want the sales team to handle any queries about placing an advert. Even simple technical questions, such as the size of adverts, should be answered by the sales team so they have a chance to start talking to the buyer. The technical team will know the answer to factual questions but can't follow up their reply later with sales patter and promotional information.

If the website is going to help serve existing customers it needs to be a real part of the business. It makes the company look fractured and demonstrates a lack of commitment to the Internet if employees in a small business don't know what's on the website or how it works. Customers are less likely to embrace a site which the company is clearly running only as a sideline.

Summary

Customers visiting your website should be invited to e-mail you any questions, so that you can begin to make contact and reassure them about your service levels. You can do this best by being prompt and accurate in your replies, and benchmarking your response against leading consumer sites.

Software can help or hinder your aim. Autoresponders enable you to send a reassuring, immediate reply. But software for putting fancy formatting into e-mails can make it slower to download and unreadable on some e-mail programs. Keep e-mails simple and use spacing, capital letters and keyboard symbols such as asterisks and dashes to enhance the message.

Agree preventative action with the team to make sure that you don't bring viruses into the business and don't smear the business reputation by perpetuating myths or sending jokes. Agree too what personal use of the Internet and the e-mail system is acceptable.

It is possible to offer customer service while visitors are visiting the website using standard chat programs or software dedicated to customer service such as Humanclick. Customer service online won't replace your existing channels, but it will give you an opportunity to open more conversations with customers and to serve them more quickly.

Make sure that the service you offer from your website is integrated with the company. The whole team should know enough about the website to help customers who are best served with it and any website-dedicated employees must know when to pass on e-mails to other departments. Your customer service messages must be consistent, however they are delivered.

Promoting your website

Your website will falter if you have poor content or
impenetrable design, but it will die if you don't promote it

Introduction

Your website will falter if you have poor content or impenetrable design, but it will die if you don't promote it. Whatever your business goal, the website's success depends on getting your intended audience to visit the site.

You're trying to introduce your future customers to your business, so if you're going to delegate the promotion, it must be to someone who knows your industry intimately. You might outsource some jobs, such as registering with search engines, but must still take control of the promotional message and ensure consistency across the business.

Successful websites will invest at least as much time in promoting the site as they did in creating it. It's a continuous process: as new pages are added to the site, they too must be registered with search engines. As new product lines become available, there's an opportunity for press coverage in new magazines. Don't dismiss website promotion as a one-off job. You've got to keep bringing new customers to the site if the business it generates is to grow.

This chapter shows how you can reach customers through non-Internet promotions, how you can reach them online, and how you can get them to return. It also discusses viral marketing and how to use e-mail ethically to promote your business.

Get the content right

You've already won half the battle if your website has information your future customers need or want. You just need to tell them about the site and why they should visit it. They'll want to go. Just make sure that you explain the benefits to them of visiting the website everywhere you promote it.

Don't forget you can promote different sections of your website to different people, giving each audience a different reason to visit the site. If you have several target audiences, you can create different pages on your website to cater for each and promote them separately.

If there is no content of general interest on your website and it's all plugging your business, you can only promote the website as somewhere to learn about your company. That way you'll only attract visitors who are interested in doing business with you already, missing the opportunity to start building a relationship with other potential customers. See Chapter 2 for ideas about content you can put on your website to attract and keep potential customers.

Choosing the right promotional methods

Internet myth search engines are all you need

Website owners often think search engine listings are the key to success and this myth is perpetuated by services that claim to get your site to the top of the rankings.

It isn't true. Search engines are like telephone directories. A listing in the phone book gives potential customers a way to reach you and most people would agree that they reach for the phone directory first when they need to track down a new company. But that doesn't mean that most customers a business deals with will come from that phone book.

In the same way, people will use search engines almost always to find new sites. But if your website is fulfilling its potential, a minority of your traffic will come from being listed.

A report by Statmarket (www.statmarket.com) in December 2000 revealed that links from other websites bring 46.13 per cent of traffic to websites, while 47.01 per cent comes from visitors going straight to the site using bookmarks or typing in the website address. Search engines account for only 6.86 per cent of visitors across websites worldwide.

How do people reach websites?

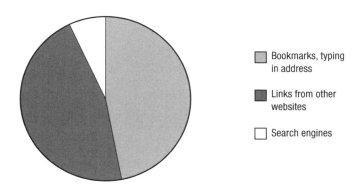

Bookmarks, typing in address

Links from other websites

Search engines

Only a minority of your visitors will come from search engines, according to data from Websidestory's Statmarket.com, an authority on global Internet user trends

Data courtesy of Websidestory

Although there are variations between industry sectors, the trend shows that you can't depend on search engines to deliver all the traffic your site should be getting. Search engine registration is important, but you can't afford to let it dominate your promotion. You should use all the other promotional channels that will reach your target audience too.

Real-world promotion

Online promotion depends on customers looking for the type of information you're providing. You're dependent on them either discovering you through a link on a related site, through an advert or in a search engine listing.

But many of your potential customers won't spend enough time online to go exploring and might log on only to check out a few sites they've read about or had recommended to them by friends.

By creating awareness of your website in the real world, you can reach out to these people.

Using existing customer contact

The good news is that you already own a lot of free advertising space. Each time you come into contact with your customers, on paper or in person, you have a chance to promote your website to them. This will be most help growing your company if your site aims to increase the business you get from existing customers or to cut the cost of dealing with them.

Here are some of the places you have free advertising space for your website:

- on the outside of your premises or on your windows;
- inside your premises – posters on the wall, labels on the counter, stickers on the floor;
- on the side and back of your vans or lorries;
- on your invoices or receipts;
- on your product packaging;
- on brochures and catalogues, job quotes and price estimates;
- in local newspaper adverts, telephone directory adverts and radio adverts. This is an opportunity to bring strangers to your website using your company's existing promotion. Often customers will be more willing to visit your website than make the commitment of phoning you and you're able to provide much more information than you can fit in the advert;
- in your newsletters;
- on your envelopes, letter heads and business cards;
- in the message on your telephone answering machine;
- on every e-mail you send out. Most e-mail programs will let you add an automatic footnote at the bottom of each message you send. This so-called 'signature' is text that tells recipients who you are and how to contact you. Include the website address here. Here's an example of how an e-mail might end with a signature shown below the four dashes:

Many thanks for your order inquiry. I've attached the estimate you requested, but please get in touch if you need any further information before confirming the order.

I look forward to hearing from you in the near future.

Best regards,
Jake

Jake Sinclair

Director
Fictional Innovations Company

Phone +1 555 5555
E-mail jsinclair@examplewebsitecompany.com

Order online to save money: www.examplewebsitecompany.com

Getting press coverage

Your site's just launched: you've got a news story. Magazines and newspapers exist to tell their readers about news and some will even dedicate sections to covering important websites. All you need to do is send them a press release with the information they need.

Make it easy for journalists to see why their readers will be interested in your website. They aren't interested in the fact that you've launched a site (who are you anyway?), they're interested in what their readers can now do that they couldn't do before. Stories can be built around superlatives – being the first, the last, the biggest or the fastest to do something – as long as these claims are substantiated and are not just hype.

There are often many different angles on the same story for different magazines. Don't try to use a standard press release for every magazine. Customize what you send to what the readers of each publication are interested in. Remember though that the goal is to get website visitors who will become customers, not to get heaps of press cuttings. Don't waste time on publications whose readers aren't a strong match with your intended website audience.

Tips for writing press releases

- Send the press release as an unformatted e-mail. (see Chapter 8 for more on e-mail presentation).

- The press release headline must briefly summarize the story, making it clear how it is relevant to the publication's readers. Stronger headlines use active language (boy meets girl) rather than passive (girl is met by boy) and structure the sentence as 'who is doing what to whom'.

- When researching any article, journalists will want to know who has done what, when, where, why and how. Include important details in the first paragraph. Which order they appear in the first paragraph will depend on what is the most important aspect of the story to the readers you are targeting.

- Press releases often conclude with 'notes to editors', where a company background can help writers to put a website into context and where unfamiliar terms can be explained in more detail.

- Remind editors to print the website address. Not all editors know enough about the web to realize that this is what makes the story work for readers.

- Include a phone number and e-mail address and invite editors to contact you for further information or a telephone interview. Don't be afraid to ask more about the magazine before answering so that you can ensure your answers are relevant to its readers.

- Including a picture can increase your chances of coverage, but ask before e-mailing any digital images. If they're good enough quality, they will be big files.

- Be concise. Journalists will skim read your first paragraph for relevance. Don't bury your story in the middle of the press release.

- Where possible, approach journalists by name who you know will have an interest in your news based on other stories they've written.

- Include quotes from senior team members but use them to say something interesting to readers, not just how delighted you are about the website launch. It might seem cruel, but readers don't care how you feel about your work.

Some Internet newswire services will (at a price) include your press release in their daily mailing to journalists who have voluntarily signed up. This can be a good way to try to generate extra interest after you've made a personal approach to the most important publications. Write a press release with the broadest possible appeal and don't just shop on price. Ask how subscribers are accredited if the newswire claims they are all journalists.

Advertising in the press and on the radio

If your website offers a new mass market service, advertising the site in the media can be a good way to spread awareness. The better you can identify your potential customers and match their profile with the media's audience, the more effective the advertising will be.

You have more control over the message than you do with press promotions, but you have to pay for it. Don't invest in advertising until you've exhausted the free promotional outlets. Create special offers or special welcome pages for each advert so you can track which ones are effective at delivering visitors and ultimately paying customers.

Promoting your website online

Websurfers can find your website by following a link or seeing its entry in a search engine and they don't need to remember your website address or even know about your business to begin with. You're just a click away, and the more roads that run into your website, the more visitors you'll be able to welcome.

Success with search engines

Most search engines index the Internet by visiting websites and following the links in them, keeping track of the titles of web pages and recording keywords as they go. These programs, known as 'spiders' because they crawl the web, might eventually stumble across your website by following a link from another site. But you can't rely on this.

Search engines often invite you to tell them about your site so that they can index it. Go to the search engine's homepage and follow the link to 'Add URL', 'Add your site' or 'Register URL'. You'll see a form to enter your website and e-mail addresses (and sometimes other details) and the search engine will add your details to the spider's in-tray. Some engines index in days, others take months.

Search engines pride themselves on delivering the best results for each query. But webmasters will often try to subvert the system and artificially inflate their importance. There's no point being on page five of the search results because no one ever gets that far. They either find what they need sooner or they try better search keywords. Search engines are being refined all the time to weed out sites that cheat and manipulate the rankings.

Here are some of the ways that search engines rank websites:

- Northern Light: indexes the first 200 words and the page title.

- Lycos: compiles its own summary of the web page.

- Google and Excite: prioritize sites with more links going to them.

- Direct Hit: ranks sites according to how many people visit them.

- Ask Jeeves: a human operator visits the site to check its suitability (Ask Jeeves also partners with other search engines from time to time to host their search results as well as its own).

- Goto: ranks sites according to how much they pay to be listed against the search keyword entered.

Directories are different. They're edited by people and the websites are organized by subject category. Yahoo and the Open Directory (at www.dmoz.org) are examples. To get listed in these, you have to find the page that your website belongs on by searching through the categories and then request that your site is added there. You'll be asked for a description and keywords. Any keywords you include in your web pages are ignored.

An entry in the Open Directory can be especially valuable because anybody can add the Open Directory (or any bit of it) to their own website for free, so you can find that sites you don't know about start linking to you. The directory also underpins many popular search engines when they don't have a keyword match in their own database.

Technology tips: optimizing your website for search engines

- Don't let your designers guess what search engine keywords you'd like your site to appear under. Tell them. Be as specific as you can with your keywords – remember, you're competing with tens of thousands of other sites, so the more unique your phrasing, the better your chances of a high ranking and a relevant customer referral if someone searches for that phrase. Think about what customers might search for and be careful of any keyword choices influenced by experience in your business that customers wouldn't have.

- Each web page has a title. This appears in the strip at the top of the browser when you visit that page and it's what goes in the favourites or bookmarks list if you want to bookmark the page. Most search engines will use this text to link to your site as well, so it needs to uniquely describe that page and what your business does. Put the most important bits of the description at the start of the title. Include your search keywords in the title to increase your ranking.

- Examples of good titles include 'Your Company Name homepage: US shoe retailers'; 'Shoe industry news from Your Company Name'.

- Bad titles (and they might seem stupid, but they pop up surprisingly often) include 'Welcome to our homepage'; 'Latest news'; 'Index.htm'; 'The world's best implementer of leading technologies to...' (runs out of space).

- Meta tags provide information to search engines which is hidden from page visitors. Each web page can have a description meta tag that includes a couple of sentences which search engines can use to describe the site together with the title. Include your keywords here and make sure the description makes sense. Don't pack it with guffy 'best company in the world' hype because people don't search for that. Think of the benefits your customers are looking for. When people see this description they will be just a click away from your website, so make it appealing to your potential customers.

- Meta tags can also specify keywords that are relevant to the page. You can add a list of keywords under which you would like your page to be found. Order the list from the most important to the least important. Include phrases such as 'shoe shop, shoe store', but don't repeat any one word more than three times. If search engines think you're trying to hype your ranking, they'll banish you.

- Make sure the keywords, description and title on each page reflect that page, and don't just use the same tags across the whole site. Remember that many search engines will index your entire site when you only tell them about your homepage, and visitors can arrive at any page of your site. Search engines usually set a limit on how many keywords per page they'll index, but don't limit how many different pages they'll index.

- Consider including common mis-spellings and international variants of important keywords.

- Want to make sure that your designers have copied the keywords correctly and there aren't any typing errors in them? Go to your website. If you're using Microsoft Internet Explorer, click on View at the top of the screen and choose Source. In Netscape Navigator click on View at the top of the screen and select Page Source (or hold down the CTRL key and press U). A window will pop up that shows the code behind the website. At the top of this code, you should see <TITLE> and <META>. These are the bits that tell search engines that use them about your page. The META line that says name="description" is your description and the line that says name="keywords" is your list of keywords, separated by commas, with the most important at the start.

- Remember, not all search engines can cope with frames and none can index text that's in a picture. (See Chapter 5 for more on what makes a good website design.)

- Include a sprinkling of the keywords on your site in your text. You might think that if it was important it would already be there. But this chapter mentions the words 'website promotion' only four times and has more than 9,000 words on the subject. Repeat your keywords without making the text too contrived. If you overdo it, search engines might suspect a scam and ban your site.

- Make sure your text counts from the start. Don't waste time welcoming visitors to your website and telling them when your company was established. Get straight to your keyword-laden business.

- Don't submit your site to any given search engine more often than monthly.

- If you have a big site with diverse content, submit different pages from your site to search engines unless they ask you not to. Don't submit multiple pages to directories.

Internet myth submit your site to 3,000 search engines

The figure varies, but the service is the same: you go to one site and for a fee (or sometimes for free) it will register your website with thousands of search engines, saving you the time visiting them individually. The problem is that after the top 20 or so search engines, there's a huge drop off in the amount of traffic you'll get from them. And all the traffic from search engines combined will bring only a small proportion of your potential customers.

These submission services will often bump up their total of search engines and directories with so-called 'free for all' or FFA links pages. These are pages where anyone visiting a website can leave behind a link for their website. There's usually a rolling chart of the 20 or so most recent entries in each category (e.g. business, music, personal homepages). New entrants bump the old ones off the bottom. These pages can deliver short bursts of traffic if your site attracts surfers who are happy casually clicking around the Internet. The price you pay for inclusion on an FFA page is in junk mail. You'll be buried in it if you give the site your real e-mail address, but can easily set up a free sacrificial e-mail account for the purpose of promoting your site and collecting related junk mail. Given how quickly pages are squeezed off an FFA page, and the lack of control over where links appear, these aren't worth the time unless you have a compelling proposition to offer the mass market.

Sometimes search engine submission programs fail and they rarely offer you the transparency you need to see whether your submission has worked or not. You don't want to sacrifice traffic from the top ten search engines for the sake of half an hour's work submitting to each of them by hand. The best approach is to submit to the most important search engines the slow way, visiting each one and adding your site individually. Wait a month, then run a free or cheap automatic submission once in a while as a bonus.

Paying to be in search engines

The Internet is growing too fast for many search engines to keep up with, so they are starting to charge websites to be included. The charges fall into these categories:

- payment for reviewing the website: No guarantee you'll get in, but you'll jump the queue for a prompt review if you pay up;

■ payment for inclusion: you have to pay to appear in the directory or search engine. This is often used by industry directories;

■ payment to appear against keywords: you pay for a prominent position when certain search keywords are entered;

■ payment when a keyword search brings visitors: you specify your keywords and pay for each visitor that comes to your site following a search using those keywords.

The keyword searches (available at Google and Goto) are worth experimenting with given the small amounts of money involved. Sites bid for ranking against the keywords, with bids starting as low as one cent. Aim to be on the first page of results, but not necessarily the first result. The extra expense often isn't justified and if you're paying for each visit you might find that listings above yours in the results will filter out those who are only curious or who used the wrong keywords.

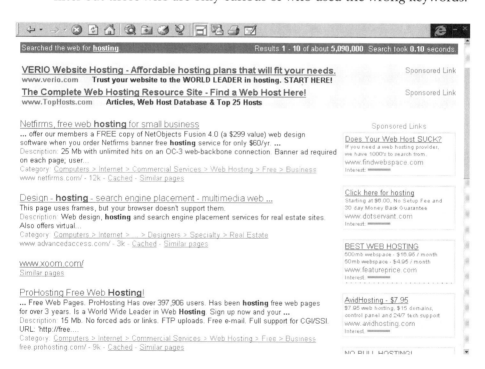

This screenshot shows the search results from Google.com after searching for 'web hosting'. The unpaid search results appear on the left and dominate the screen. Adverts, triggered by the search keywords used, appear in boxes down the right-hand side and in horizontal bars across the top. Adverts are labelled 'Sponsored Links' and appear on a coloured background

Screenshot courtesy of Google Inc.

If you're paying for inclusion, be sure that it's worth it. The value of your entry in a directory or search engine depends on how well it is promoted to and used by your target audience. Search engines that rank sites purely according to how rich they are lack credibility when bad sites buy a high entry. Such search engines often rely on the fact that visitors don't know it's going on or don't know how to use a different search engine.

A final word on search engines

It's a paradise for scamsters: all these confusing search engines and all these sites jostling for prominence in them. Some people will claim they can get you to the top of the search engines and they have a foolproof technique. Sometimes they will have, until the spiders learn about it. But there's always a cost involved and it's rarely worth it. Don't forget that only a minority of your visitors will come from search engines if you're promoting your website properly.

Remember, the real value of a listing depends on the keywords you use attracting potential customers and not on the number of visitors you get. You can add new content to your site and promote that to attract a different visitor demographic – money is better invested in new content and giving visitors new reasons to visit the site than in spoofing search engines.

Attracting links

There are several advantages to persuading other websites to link to you.

- A website endorses your site by linking to it. Visitors expect to find your site relevant and know that the referring site has vetted yours to make sure it's worth them visiting. By contrast, few search engines hand-check a site before listing it and they get confused by words with multiple meanings (such as bridge: is that a river crossing? A card game? A bit of a song? A part of your nose?).

- A link suggests a website that visitors might not have considered searching for but would be interested in now they know it exists and it's just a click away.

- Some search engines use the number of links to a site and where they come from to rank a site's importance. If one site has a lot of links going to it, the search engine assumes that it is a respected authority on its subject. Its outbound links are more credible as result, so sites that it links to also benefit from a higher ranking. Google.com has been the pioneer in using this technique.

There's a price to pay for links, though, and that price is measured in time and visitors. Every visitor who follows a link is leaving the site hosting it. Any site linking to you is going to want a link back so they benefit as well. You'll need to send some of your visitors their way, and you'll need to invest time in keeping your links page up to date and seeking new link partners.

Use search engines and directories to find sites you want to exchange links with. You could also use the search engine altavista.com to find sites that are linking to your competitors. Enter 'link:' plus your competitor's website address in the search box, and you'll get a list of sites linking to them.

Don't limit yourself to company websites. Amateur websites and online magazines can have a well-defined audience, plenty of casual visitors and strong content. These sites are developed out of a love for them, and their creators often spend a lot of time on content and promotion, far more than a business could afford. (See Chapter 2 for tips on thinking laterally in seeking link partners.)

Don't compromise on website quality in your link partners. You're going to have to link back to them, and your credibility will suffer if you recommend a site that stinks. You don't have to be as ruthless judging presentation as you do with your site, but you must insist on worthwhile content.

The best opportunities are where websites already have a links page set up that you can join. E-mail the webmasters who manage the sites you'd like to get links from. Tell them a little about your website and ask them if they'd like to exchange links. Suggest the link description you'd like to see, so you can give readers a reason to click on the link.

Before asking sites to link to you, however, be confident that you've got content that their readers will like. If you've got a site that just promotes your company, you're asking link partners to endorse your

9 Promoting your website

business and nobody will recommend a company to their customers just because the company asked them to.

If you've published information that their visitors (your potential customers) need to know, they can recommend the website as a source of information or entertainment to their visitors. Don't waste time trying to get links from sites that aren't relevant to your content (irrespective of how relevant they are to your business).

There are shareware programs that will search the web for websites featuring a keyword or links to your competitors' sites. The programs then e-mail the webmasters of these sites with a standardized message asking for a link to your site. These programs aren't recommended. The e-mails read like junk mail that struck lucky on its relevance this time and are trashed accordingly. It's better to contact webmasters personally and introduce yourself. Even though we use machines to keep in touch, people do business with people, not bulk mailing software.

You might find that potential link partners stumble across your site, so make it easy for them to link their web pages to yours by including instructions on how to do it and adverts they can put on their site to bring you visitors. If you have a database or a search engine on your site, try offering a box that webmasters can put on their site so their visitors can enter your site by doing a search. If you're selling shoes, you could let visitors enter their shoe size in a form, then click a button to visit your site and find all the latest deals in their size. If you're selling films, you could provide a box for visitors to enter their favourite actor, so that they enter your site to see their star's movies on offer.

Amateur homepage authors might stumble across this link and should be encouraged to link to your site if they want to. If websites don't meet your standards for a return link, there's no reason to deter one-way links into your site if someone wants to make them.

Don't forget too that reciprocal traffic isn't the only reason you'll want to include links on your website. Chapter 2 shows how links can make your site more attractive to visitors.

Technology tips: linking

- You can open links in a new window by clicking on them with the right mouse button (instead of the left) and selecting the option from the pop-up menu if you're using a PC, or by clicking and holding down the button if you're using a Macintosh. If you tell your visitors this, you can keep the ones who aren't finished with your site yet while letting them follow your links.

- You can make links from your site automatically open in a new window so that when visitors have finished looking around the linked site your site is still there on screen. You should warn people if you're going to do this with links because it can be irritating and can cause confusion. Sites that are reluctant to link to you might be more willing if you suggest this idea because they don't so much lose visitors as lend them to you.

- You can make linked sites appear inside a frame so that there's a permanent link back to your site on screen. This can be annoying and linked sites might have a legal case against you if they object (see Chapter 10 for more on linking and the law). If you do this, give visitors the option to get rid of the panel containing your link.

Syndicating your content to other websites

You can encourage websites to link to you by offering them something of value, typically either content or money.

Syndication systems enable you to give your headlines, stories or other regularly updated content to other websites. These sites harvest the latest information from your site by using special links. The benefit to you is that you get links on other sites that pull people straight into your stories using the hottest news headlines. The sites hosting your headlines are enhanced with timely information, even if the full stories are available only by clicking to your site where the full story is.

If you consider your website to be an online magazine, this could be a good strategy for you, but without a commitment to regularly updated content, syndication is useless. Webmasters won't thank you for making their sites look neglected because of your old news.

Isyndicate (www.isyndicate.com) offers syndication services to websites. Clients pay a setup fee and pay for each time someone visits their site. Content can be sold on to other sites or given away.

If you plan it from the start, it might be more cost effective to have your own syndication mechanism designed into your website, although you can only syndicate to webmasters who find your website first. One strength of using an intermediary like Isyndicate is that they will be able to offer your services to sites that have never heard of you and your content will be listed alongside that of well-known newspapers and broadcasters.

Operating affiliate programmes

Affiliate programmes are where you pay websites to link to you, either paying for each visitor they send you or paying a percentage of the sales value from referred visits. (See Chapter 6 for more information on how affiliate programmes work.)

If you have to pay other sites to link to your editorial content, it suggests that either you've got the wrong content or you've got the wrong link partners. Small businesses that aren't selling from their website will be better off investing in their content instead of affiliate programmes and exchanging links with other non-competing websites for free.

Most small businesses should avoid setting up pay-per-click programmes. They don't reflect the value of a customer, so sites are encouraged to send you visitors irrespective of how closely they match who you want to reach. The rates you can afford to pay for someone to look at your homepage in the hope that they will browse deeper will deter serious websites from participating.

If your site sells directly, you can pay commission to reward affiliate partners only when they refer a buying customer to you. The cost of customer acquisition is low and you usually pay commission only on the first visit because next time customers will come straight to you. Partner websites are rewarded for the quality of the customers they send and are likely to create content on their site that encourages visitors to buy your products, instead of just urging them to visit your site.

You can also pay per lead, where you reward partners for visitors who follow their link to your website and then join your mailing list or express their interest in another way. This can be effective for high-value goods or services that you can't sell online.

You could create your own affiliate system, but there are well-established intermediaries including Commission Junction (www.cj.com), Linkshare (www.linkshare.com) and Befree (befree.com) which will manage affiliate programs on your behalf. They take a cut of the rate you pay your affiliates in return for automating links and visitor tracking. These systems also have software that tries to identify webmasters clicking on their own links to increase payments.

However you run your programme, you'll need the resources to manage inquiries and will need to control your cash flow so that you can pay affiliate partners promptly. The chances are that these people are also your customers, and the fact they're linking to you shows that they have contact with other customers, so it's important to be professional.

Many affiliate programmes create bad feeling by cutting back their rates once affiliates have done the work of implementing links. You'll get more loyalty from your link partners if you operate a stable programme paying a lower rate than you will from a programme with rates that start generously and plummet later.

Low payment rates will breed disloyalty among affiliates, but if the rates are set too high, you could lose more money the more business you get. To decide what you can afford, work out the average value of a visitor to your website. If visitors typically view five adverts and you get ten cents for each, you know that you can't afford to pay more than 50 cents on average to attract a visitor and break even. If visitors spend $5 on average in your business (on the site, on the phone, or in person) and you make $1 profit out of that, you erode the profit completely with commission levels as high as 20 per cent on website sales or pay-per-customer rates of more than $1. Chapter 11 tells you more about how to measure visitor behaviour and Chapter 6 tells you more about the different ways you can pay affiliates (pay per click, pay per lead and commission).

Webrings

Webrings enable sites on the same subject to join in a chain. On each site, there's a box with a link to the next site in the chain and the previous site. Visitors to one site can then easily work their way through related sites. They can also skip sites and access a directory of all the sites in the ring.

It's a good way to attract well-targeted visitors, both through links on neighbouring sites and through the directory of all the sites.

Websites usually add themselves to the ring and then another site in the ring checks that the website is relevant and authorizes the ring membership.

All the links go through a central website that refers visitors to the site they need, so if your neighbours change, the central website will divert visitors without you needing to update your links.

One drawback is that you can't control who you're linking to in the chain, but all sites are vetted by other ring members or the ring manager before being admitted to the ring so the risk is minimal. The biggest problem with webrings is that they fracture. Member sites sometimes greedily delete their webring box so that they get visitors but don't give any away or sometimes websites move so that visitors find sites missing. Don't be afraid of sharing traffic. Visitors will leave your site only if you're not offering what they need.

The leading webring operator is at www.webring.org, where you can find a relevant webring to join or can start your own. You can also ask your web design team to custom-create a webring program for you or to use some off-the-shelf software to build one.

Advertising your website online

One way to tell people about your website on the Internet is by advertising on sites that are relevant. But you can't expect to get many customers unless you're spending a lot on advertising: for every visitor you receive you could be paying for several hundred visitors to ignore your advert. You'll be expected to pay for each impression, but will get a measurable benefit only when a visitor comes to the site.

That doesn't mean links must be followed to be valuable. They can still spread awareness. Design your adverts to tell people quickly who you are, what you do and what your website address is for if they want to visit later.

Some advertising channels are rewarding surfers for watching adverts by paying them in money, free software or in charitable donations on their behalf. These networks are good for society – they give people a free way to help charities and give companies an easy way to help them, they make software available to people who might not otherwise be able to afford it, and they transform advertising into a paying entertainment medium. These channels can help to build a strong brand online. But whenever you place adverts hoping to get website visitors, be careful about what motivates people to click on them. You want to attract visitors who might become customers, not visitors who have been bribed to visit a certain number of websites when yours happens to come along.

Companies with global consumer products can afford to assume every web surfer is a potential customer and so can place their adverts without much targeting. But as a small business, it will be more effective to ally your adverts with content that will interest your potential customers on other websites. The more narrowly you can home in on potential customers, the more effective your adverts will be.

If you're advertising on portals, aim for those that are dedicated to your industry or sponsor appropriate categories in their directory. If you're advertising on websites, look for the sites you want to appear on and try speaking to them directly about placing an advert on their site. They'll be able to tell you how many unique visitors they have and by dealing direct you can negotiate deals outside the usual pay-per-impression or pay-per-click structures.

When choosing an advertising network that coordinates adverts across lots of different sites, look for one that categorizes websites. The more narrow the categories, the more likely it is that those who see your advert will be interested in your products and services. Smaller categories means fewer viewers, but you should choose quality over quantity every time.

The position of the advert on the screen can be equally important. Remember, you're paying for the advert to appear on the page, not whether or not the reader sees it, so adverts at the bottom of the page are worth much less to you than adverts at the top. Readers could read the first few paragraphs and click on to the next page without even scrolling. Some websites use pop-ups, which are adverts that appear in their own window when someone goes to a web page (often the homepage). These irritate Internet users and many close the box on reflex before it even starts downloading. If you use pop-ups, pay only for those that download fully.

The cost of advertising varies significantly. You can pay a few cents per impression on some networks of homepages, and spend thousands advertising on a major portal. If you speak to sites directly, especially other small business sites and sites run as a hobby, you may be able to form partnerships that benefit both sites without incurring huge fees.

Tips on designing adverts

- Include your domain name prominently in the advert, to spread awareness of where visitors can reach you. There's a chance they'll visit later if they're busy now, but only if they know where to go. The advert itself will often go through an advert management program and won't link straight to your site.

- Include your branding in the banner.

- You're competing with whatever readers are already looking at on screen, so give them a good reason to divert their attention.

- Make the link take visitors to a page that builds on your promotional message. Don't promise them a discount and then dump them at your homepage with no further mention of it. Make the transition smooth.

- If the advertising network lets you specify the text description that goes with your advert, write a single line offer that works in isolation. For example: 'Sample Music Company: Click here to save 20% on imported music.' Even visitors with images switched off can see your advert then.

- Optimize your advert so that it downloads quickly. The quicker it downloads, the more chance there is that visitors will see it. Don't forget to use the safe colour palette. (There's more information on using graphics in Chapter 5.)

- Animation is often used to attract attention, but don't expect visitors to sit through it like a slideshow. As soon as they see there's an advert, many readers will scroll it off the screen. By the time the advert's finished loading and announced with fanfare what it's supposed to be promoting, the visitor might not even be on the page any more. Use animation to enhance the promotional message, not postpone it.

- There are many online programs for creating banner adverts, but they often produce similar-looking and dull adverts. Beware of using tired advert templates.

Banner exchanges

Banner exchanges can be a better investment than buying advertising on other sites if you have regular visitors to your website. It works like this. You join an advertising network and display adverts on your website which the network automatically pulls from its database of members. In exchange, you get your adverts displayed on sites elsewhere in the network. Commercial adverts are also sold into the network to cover the network operator's costs and profit, so you'll have to display several adverts for each time yours is shown. Typical ratios for exchanging advert credits are 2:1 and 3:2. Some banner exchanges will let you target your advert at particular categories of website, while others are dedicated to certain business sectors and countries.

The downside of carrying advertising is that you invite your visitors to leave your site wherever adverts appear. But using the price quoted to outside companies that want to advertise on the network, the value of your advertising credits will be more than you're likely to earn through affiliate programmes and you're bringing customers into your core business.

Successful e-mail promotion

E-mail offers a cheap way to tell customers about your website and your products, but you must be careful to ensure that your e-mails are welcome. Bad e-mail promotion does more harm than good.

Junk e-mail or spam

Junk e-mail is known as spam in tribute to the Monty Python sketch where whatever you ordered in a cafe, a generous helping of spam was unavoidable. Many people open their e-mail to keep in touch with friends and are buried in a deluge of offers for impotence drugs they don't need, pornography they don't want, and mortgages for the gullible.

Databases of e-mail addresses are widely and cheaply available. They're either compiled by programs that crawl the web, ripping all the e-mail addresses out of websites, or by websites which breach their visitors' trust by selling their addresses given in good faith. Sometimes the lists will claim to be opt-in, where the people on the list have chosen to be there. But nobody signs up for unlimited junk mail.

There are several reasons not to send spam.

- Typical spam promotes pornography, miracle drugs, get-rich-quick schemes and overpriced website promotion services. You don't want to be seen in the company of dodgy businesses.

- Spam obstructs people trying to work and keep in touch with friends and family. The volume of junk e-mail being sent is becoming comparable to the phone ringing with insurance salesmen every time you want to make a call. Ferris Research (www.ferris.com) estimates that by 2005 around 40 per cent of a typical user's e-mail will be junk. People will hate you if you spam them.

- You risk disrupting your business. Sending spam is banned by most service providers. If you are reported, they will investigate and close down your e-mail address and website. Hackers will often act directly and delete your website if they can. If you're added to the junk mail filters people use to manage their e-mail, every message you send in future will go straight in the trash without even being seen. If you send enough spam, all your e-mail will be blocked from some Internet service providers.

- Sending spam is illegal in some countries and states.

When you send junk e-mail you send a clear signal that you don't care about your customers, or about marketing ethics.

Advertising in e-mail newsletters

One way to reach new customers is to advertise in a newsletter issued by another website. There are four main types of newsletter:

- **Opt-in marketing newsletters** Members choose to be on the list which exists to send them targeted advertising. Often the website they sign up at offers them 'news and special offers from carefully selected companies', but the only selection factor is how much money the advertiser is prepared to pay. The more e-mails readers receive, the less interest they will have in them.

- **Opt-in information newsletters** Readers choose to be on the list because they want to read the information in newsletters. These will be regular and might include news stories, opinion articles or other reports. The main thing is that the list itself is entertaining or useful.

- **Opt-out newsletters** People are added to a list automatically, but can choose to leave it. This is no better than junk e-mail. List members can't tell genuine offers to remove addresses from fakes, and will be unwilling to reply to the e-mail as that will prove their e-mail address works and might increase the spam they receive.

- **'Necessary evil'** People are forced to join the e-mail list to get benefits such as access to a website or a free e-book. Visitors will give the database a sacrificial e-mail address, one they use only for receiving and deleting junk mail unread. If a mailing list includes mainly free web-based e-mail providers, it shows a lack of trust or interest in being on the list.

The best approach is to choose an information newsletter that matches your customers' interests and insert a text advert in it. You can never be sure that they'll have time to read the newsletter, but that's no worse than not knowing how many people see your newspaper advert. You can at least be confident that the advert will appear in the context of a welcome e-mail.

If you have a special offer, it might be effective to send a message to an opt-in marketing database or a 'necessary evil' database, but make sure that the message makes it clear to recipients how they got on the database. You might find your adverts draw more attention if they're presented as a 'Special offer in partnership with' the website that owns the list if it's a respected brand.

Chapter 8 includes more information on using e-mail to keep in touch with your customers. See page 170 for tips on using your own newsletter to bring customers back.

Discussion groups

E-mail discussion groups will usually frown upon adverts, but you can still develop an awareness of your site there. The best thing is to join a discussion group relevant to your customer base and contribute to discussions with helpful answers where possible, including a link to your site in your e-mail signature with each reply. Take the opportunity to tell people about your content where it answers a question, but don't just ask people to visit the site. You can find appropriate groups by searching on the web, or going to www.liszt.com (a search engine for lists) or sites such as www.groups.yahoo.com (a site that hosts lots of lists).

Newsgroups are discussion groups that use the Internet but not necessarily the web, and use special newsreader software to send and receive messages. Because these forums aren't dependent on any one website to attract their readers, they can have a far greater reach than discussion groups linked to one website. The newsgroup archives will keep your message available long after it was posted as well. There's a website that will let you access newsgroups at www.deja.com, which is owned by Google.com.

Whether you are using e-mail discussion groups or newsgroups, the trick to increasing your website traffic is to participate in the online community and share information. Take the opportunity to learn from your customers and to hear about what your competitors are doing. If you're interested only in website traffic, discussion groups are an inefficient use of your time.

Loyalty schemes

Beenz.com was the pioneer in this market, but there are several virtual loyalty schemes that websites can join. Customers can collect points by shopping, visiting or registering at certain websites. When they have earned enough points, they can spend them at participating online stores. The loyalty schemes establish a virtual economy in points, with websites that award points paying the scheme operator for them and shops that accept them being paid for those they take. These schemes enable sites to give away something that costs only a few cents to them but has a greater collectable value to the customer.

Dedicated points-collectors might come to your site just looking to grow their credits, but as long as you use the points to motivate behaviour that helps your business, every visitor counts. The arguments are similar to those for affiliate programmes: pay a modest incentive for sales and you can't go wrong. Pay for every visitor and you need to be certain you're making enough money from advertising.

Awards

Awards are mentioned here because there are so many of them online, but they're not recommended.

Very few website awards are worth having, at least for promotional reasons. If you get an award that recognizes your excellence in the industry and is given against stiff competition by a reputed industry body, it might encourage customers to trade with you. But awards where you are listed as the 'best site of the day' somewhere with a link to your site won't deliver enough traffic to justify the hassle of finding award sites and getting nominated. The next day, your site is long forgotten. Awards are usually seen on amateur websites where webmaster pride is the only motivator.

Bringing visitors back

If a customer bookmarks your website, it's more likely that they'll come back later. You don't have to do anything except remind visitors to add the site to their favourites or bookmarks folder. Whether they do so or not will depend on how useful they found your site, but it's the repeat visitors who are most likely to become your more valuable customers.

If you've created a portal, encourage visitors to make it their default start page. Provide instructions for this and for bookmarking the site.

In Chapter 2 we also considered content you can offer to remind visitors to come back, such as screensavers and wallpaper. Anything you can do that gives you a presence on the user's computer is a good idea. You can't guarantee that people will come back regularly, but if you've got a good page title you can at least remind them of your site's existence each time they look at bookmarks near it in their list. When they need your site, they'll be reminded of where they need to go.

Publishing an e-mail newsletter

One way to bring visitors back into your website is to e-mail them to tell them what's new. The challenge is to convince them to give you their e-mail address in the first place. They must trust that you're not going to sell their address to junk e-mailers and that you're not going to keep sending them nagging 'come see our site again' e-mails that don't add any value.

You can create a newsletter to tell your readers about new information on your website, special offers or new products. Send the newsletter regularly, but not so often that it becomes an intrusion.

The technology for running a newsletter is simple. Websites such as www.listbot.com will do all the work of managing your mailing list if you link to them and there are lots of off-the-shelf programs you can have integrated into your website. They'll let your site visitors join your list automatically, will verify the address is valid and will give you the mechanism to e-mail the whole group in one go.

You can start the list by inviting your existing customers to join it. After that it will grow steadily as more people visit the website and hear about your newsletter.

Remind forgetful readers how they got on your mailing list in each newsletter you send so that they don't think you're spamming them and tell them how to unsubscribe each time. Make it as easy as possible (just sending an e-mail is best) and tell them how to contact you if they can't unsubscribe themselves.

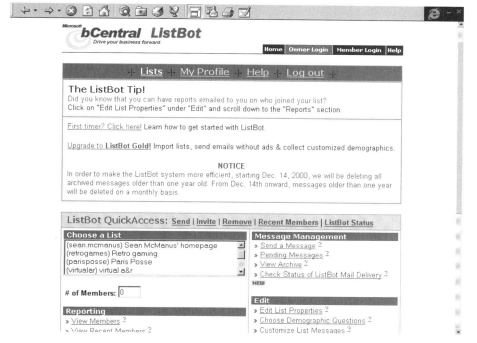

It's easy for anyone to operate a mailing list through www.listbot.com

Screenshot reprinted by permission from Microsoft Corporation

Viral marketing (including e-cards and referral mechanisms)

All over the world, people recognize the same jokes and the same music. And a lot of this is because friends tell each other jokes and recommend albums to each other. On the Internet good ideas can spread like diseases, and this is the premise of viral marketing. It's been said that you can connect any two people in the world through six acquaintances, so powerful ideas can quickly take hold.

You can harness online word of mouth in several ways.

■ Suggest to visitors that they recommend your website to a friend. If they appreciate what you've created and know someone else who will like it, they will refer potential customers to you.

■ Give visitors a mechanism for e-mailing individual articles from your website to a friend. That way your stories can reach visitors

171

who don't even come to the site, and each e-mail can tell them where to come next time they need similar information. Let customers add their own messages to the outgoing e-mail. If a friend sends you an article and explains why you should read it, the chances are you will. It's best to just delete the e-mail addresses you obtain in this way straight after you've sent the message and make it clear that's what you do. Customers will be wary if you start adding them to mailing lists or storing addresses for any other reason.

- Encourage customers to forward your e-mail newsletters to friends. Make sure there are instructions for how to join the mailing list with each newsletter that goes out.

- Offer electronic postcards (also known as e-cards) from your website. Visitors choose a picture and write a message. Their friends receive an e-mail with a link where they can see the picture and read the message on your website. Electronic postcards have the added advantage that they can be an enticing enough feature to draw visitors to the website in the first place.

- Give customers an incentive to recommend your business to their friends. You could offer them a discount voucher for each new customer they send you and give new customers a discount off their first purchase. That way you can leverage your existing customer database to bring in new business at a low cost.

- Create software, songs or wallpaper that customers will want to send to their friends. Make it easy for them to do so and give other websites permission to distribute your programs. You could also create electronic books about any aspect of your industry. These can have a high perceived value but incur no costs apart from those related to writing them.

CASE STUDIES

Good ideas are catching

Moreover's news feeds are a good example of viral marketing. The company (at www.moreover.com) offers blocks of news headlines from all over the web that you can integrate into your website. Each block of headlines includes a link inviting readers to 'add headlines to your website'. Website owners who like what they see can follow the link to put the same (or their choice of another set of) headlines on their own website. With each website that signs up to deliver Moreover's headlines, the company spreads its brand and its links further throughout the web and starts delivering its message to 'add headlines to your site' to a whole new audience. The site signed up more than 100,000 sites in around 19 months.

Zthing (www.zthing.com) is a humour site that launched in 1999 to publish cartoons, games, mini-movies and song parodies. The website's parody of a popular Britney Spears song in 2000 was sent to 100,000 mailing list members by e-mail and resulted in nearly 650,000 visitors to the website within three months. More than 225,000 of the visitors were referred using an e-mail recommendation sent from the website by a friend and many others visited as a result of forwarded e-mails.

Summary

Website promotion needs to permeate your whole business. There will be activities you undertake for the first time, such as registering with search engines and possibly advertising on other websites. But you should also make sure that your site is promoted widely throughout your company on 'free' advertising space. Tell receptionists the address and when they should refer customers to it. Ask sales assistants to chat to customers about the site.

If you've got the content right, other websites will want to link to yours and customers will want to come back. Make it easy by telling them how to do so.

Don't waste time on ineffective promotion. Target your customers as narrowly as you can and create a promotional message that will give them a good reason to visit the site. Use it everywhere you use your domain name: make your potential customers feel like they're missing out if they don't visit.

Promotion doesn't stop after the site's launched. You'll need to keep bringing previous visitors back to the site and keep telling your new walk-in customers about it. You'll need to keep attracting strangers to your business through the website as well.

Armed with data on who's coming to your site and what they're doing there, you can repromote it to increase awareness among other target markets you need to break into. Chapter 11 discusses how to find out who's visiting.

Keeping your
website legal and ethical

It's as much a case of behaving ethically and
professionally as it is of second-guessing the legislators

Introduction

Legislation has struggled to catch up with the pace of the Internet. All of a sudden, laws that have regulated newspapers and national businesses for decades don't make sense online, where ownership of information is hard to defend and there are no geographic boundaries. Many potentially important test cases have been settled out of court, leaving litigants none the wiser about what judges believe.

When you set up your website, you become a global publisher and an international marketer. You might not be able to predict how courts will interpret some laws when applied to the web, but you can still limit your risk. The laws were all intended to restore fair play to the market and to protect consumers, so it's as much a case of behaving ethically and professionally as it is of second-guessing the legislators.

This chapter focuses on the most important issues and offers guidelines for ethical behaviour that will help to keep you out of trouble.

This doesn't constitute legal advice, and as always, it's a good investment to speak to an expert about your situation if you are concerned.

Copyright

It isn't fair if someone does all the work and someone else steals it and exploits it commercially or gives it away so that the creator can't make a living. That's why copyright law restricts the copying, distribution and publication of creative work. It embraces words, pictures, photos, songs, performances, software, website designs: virtually everything you'll want to use on your website. You'll need permission from writers, photographers or other creators to include their material on your website.

The business will own the copyright in work that employees do, but freelancers and subcontractors will keep their copyright unless you make a transfer part of a written contract.

Designers will want to keep their copyright in the website's programming so that they can re-use parts of the design in other sites, which helps to keep costs lower for everyone. There is a separate copyright in the website's look and feel. Make it part of the written contract that this copyright is assigned to you and that you can get anyone to modify the design on your behalf. If you're going to want to launch other websites with the same design, make sure that you've got clearance to do this in the contract.

Designers will often use 'royalty-free' art collections, which allow them to copy the contents as much as they want in exchange for the price of the CD Rom. Check that your design team has clearance to use any material it supplies for your site and hasn't just taken it from another site, or exceeded the licence terms of a royalty-free collection. Include a clause in your contract that they will indemnify you for any legal costs arising from any copyright infringements that they make.

The content of the website is also protected by copyright. The protection doesn't usually expire until 70 years after the author's death. Even then there can be several layers of copyright. You're free to put Shakespeare's sonnets on your website, but might not be allowed to scan a book because the page design is still protected.

If you commission a copywriter, agree a licence with them that gives you permission to use their copy on your website and anywhere else you want to use it. Writers have a right to be identified as the author of a text, but they can agree to waive this so-called moral right as part of the contract. For purely commercial writing, you should obtain a copyright assignment and moral rights waiver in writing.

If your website lets your visitors leave messages, include a clause in the terms and conditions that grants you permission to use their work for promotional use. If you have any other uses planned (such as using their material in a book), be upfront about it. Without their permission, you can't use their work.

If you hire a photographer to take shots of your team or your products for the website, be clear about where you can and can't use it. If your photos include people, you might need to get 'model release forms' signed. These protect you if the picture is used in a way that the model objects to, such as if you want to use a generic picture to illustrate an incompetent computer user.

There is no copyright in facts or ideas, but there is copyright in how those ideas are expressed.

Copyright law and linking

The Internet was built on the idea of being able to join up information wherever it is in the world with a simple link. But as soon as there were commercial interests behind the content, it became confusing.

What if a competitor linked to your site and made it look like part of theirs? What if someone linked directly to one of your images so that it appeared to be part of their website? It's not always obvious where one site ends and another begins, especially when a website links deep into another site, beyond the homepage. Lawyers have argued that a link can breach copyright law by denying a website the credit it's entitled to for its content.

Sometimes websites will frame sites they link to, so that the screen is split and there's a banner that features a link back. The success of any adverts displayed in this banner, though, depends on how long people want to read the other site. Some lawyers argue it's hijacking the branding and quality of content at another site. It can create the appearance of a partnership or an ownership of content that doesn't exist.

Make sure that your visitors know where your site begins and ends and get permission for any links that could cause visitors confusion about who owns what content. Check whether sites mind being framed or being linked to if there's any doubt. Lawyers advise companies to agree a written contract for every link on the website, but they are in the business of eliminating risks (however small they are) and few websites go to such lengths. It's always safest to link to the homepage of a site because that's where the site can introduce itself to visitors and make clear its content ownership.

If you want to link to a site using its logo, you'll need permission because the logo is protected by copyright and might also be a trade mark.

Trade marks

Trade mark law helps companies to build on their customer goodwill and reap the rewards of advertising by controlling how their promotional identity is used. A trade mark can be almost anything that distinguishes one company from another, including a brand name, a jingle or a slogan.

Check whether your domain name includes any trade marks that you don't own and be careful about what keywords you submit to search engines in your meta tags (see Chapter 9). You might be selling branded goods but the company that makes them has the exclusive right to use their trade marks to attract traffic to their website. Courts in the US have handed over domain names featuring trade marks to the trade mark holder.

It's a measure of success for some products that their names are often used in conversation to refer to the type of product, whoever it's made by. Popular trade marks include Hoover, Biro, Velcro and Nylon, but they shouldn't be used to refer to a competitor's products. A complaint on your website needs to be vetted for any brand names so that it doesn't become an undeserved attack on one company, and product descriptions should be careful not to exploit the goodwill in a rival manufacturer's brand.

One of the best-known Internet bandwagons has been domain-name trading, where people buy domain names including popular brands purely to re-sell them at a premium without ever launching a website using the name. It's a parasitic way to build a business, racing somebody to a resource they need but you don't and then charging them a premium to buy it from you. Where domain names have been registered in the hope of selling them to the company that owns the brand name in the domain, courts have been handing them over without payment. If you have to take action against websites that have registered domain names including your trade marks, start with the disputes resolution process at ICANN (Internet Corporation for Assigned Names and Numbers–www.icann.org) for '.com' domains or the national body that awards your domain name. (See Chapter 4 for more information on domain names.)

Patents

Invention is an expensive business, so patents give inventors the exclusive right to exploit their technology for 20 years. This causes something of a problem with modern technology, however – the commercial Internet has popularized so quickly that while revolutionary ideas from its infancy now seem obvious, they are still under patent. Amazon holds a patent for its one-click ordering process, for example, where returning customers can order a product by clicking on one button and the address and payment details are taken from their accounts automatically.

It might be wise to conduct a patent search if you're having interactive features custom-designed for your website. You might be able to minimize the risk by licensing off-the-shelf products for your interactive features. You might also want to include an indemnity clause in your web design contract that the designers will indemnify you for patents they infringe.

Libel

If you write something that might make readers think less of someone, you risk infringing libel law, which exists to protect personal reputations. You're free to write it if it's true, but you'll need to be able to prove it if it comes to court. Litigants can pick and choose who they sue, so it's not enough to show that it's appeared in print elsewhere without a murmur of complaint.

You can libel someone without naming them if they can still be identified, and you can even increase the chance of being sued by being more vague. If you tried to avoid naming names by saying that 'one of the board of directors is corrupt' you risk being sued by any of them who think they've been defamed and not just the one you think is crooked.

Take care that people you write about can't be confused with others who share the same name. You can limit the risk by putting people in context, for example by including their job titles and companies or home towns.

As long as your content is true and isn't malicious, you shouldn't need to worry about libel on your website. Be careful if your visitors can leave messages, though. Respond promptly to any complaints and if you have the resources, consider vetting messages before they go live. As part of your website's terms and conditions, include a disclaimer that you aren't responsible for the content of these messages.

When newspapers commit libel, anyone in the production and distribution chain can be sued for distributing it, from the printer to the shops. It's been argued that websites that link to a libellous site are also implicated for spreading the message. Vet any sites you link to and add a disclaimer that you aren't responsible for what visitors discover after leaving your site.

Rating content

The Internet community has so far deterred censorship legislation by showing that it can regulate itself.

Before being released, films are usually screened by censors who give them a rating so that children are protected from seeing scenes they shouldn't. Online, website managers can rate their own sites and embed an invisible code in the page that will tell the visitor's software what sort of content the page includes. Parents can set their child's web browser to block sites that say they carry unsuitable material.

Websites are graded for the language used, nudity and sexual content, violence, drugs, gambling and chat. These sections are broken down so that parents can allow cartoon violence but block blood and gore, or allow profanity that doesn't include sexual swear words. The content can also be flagged for medical or scientific interest, so that parents can authorize sex education or military history but block pornography and horror.

The industry standard is PICS (Platform for Internet Content Selection) and you can complete a questionnaire to get your free PICS code at the Internet Content Rating Association's website at www.icra.org. (ICRA is a successor to RSACi, Recreational Software Advisory Council on the Internet, which is still often referred to.)

Cautious parents might block all sites that don't certify themselves, so it is even worth child-friendly sites getting a rating. ICRA says that search engines intended for children will also look for PICS ratings to compile their index and that customers see sites that certify themselves as more trustworthy.

Although the ratings are often thought of as protecting children, they also help defend free speech online. Adults who object to your content can make sure they don't run the risk of seeing it by accident and so any argument they have against your right to publish the material diminishes, unless the material is illegal.

It's been said that if you followed all the restrictions on free speech worldwide, you'd have nothing left to say. But make sure that your content at least meets the standards that society expects in your target markets. If you know that your content offends some people, offer a warning before entering the site to give visitors a chance to opt out.

Accessibility

Many countries (including the UK and the US) explicitly outlaw discrimination against the disabled. How far this principle applies online hasn't been clarified by case law yet, but given how easy it is for websites to be designed to be accessible using voice readers, Braille readers or other equipment, there's a responsibility for websites to comply.

Sites that are accessible using assistive technology also tend to be easier to use for visitors using standard browsers. The guidelines in Chapter 5 will help to shape a site that works for everyone. You can test your website for any problems with accessibility using Bobby at www.cast.org/bobby. However, although the site will point out anything that's definitely wrong, it doesn't mean that the site's okay if Bobby reports no errors because it can't understand (for example) whether the alternative text behind images makes any sense, or whether all your link descriptions just say 'click here'.

Few website designers shape sites for accessibility, but it's not difficult for them to do so if you draw attention to the issues.

Junk e-mail

Junk e-mail shifts the cost of promotion from companies to the consumer without asking them first. Thousands of e-mails can be sent for the same price as a single posted letter. But consumers pay to download the junk e-mails in time and in money. Internet costs increase because of the technology needed to route all the unwanted messages. Sending junk e-mail shows disrespect for your audience.

Legislation varies worldwide, and even from state to state in the US. Some laws require messages to have 'ADV' for advertisement in the subject line. Others require a valid opt-out address so that recipients can remove themselves from the junk mail list. In some states it's an offence to send spam at all or to forge the address it appears to have come from. EU law gives people the right to say they don't want their personal data to be processed for direct marketing purposes.

Many laws represent a compromise between marketers who plead their right to free speech and consumers who argue they're being forced to pay for rubbish. But whatever the law says, people will hate you if you spam them. To keep your site ethical, don't send junk e-mail.

For more information on spam and how to use e-mail to promote your business ethically, see Chapter 9.

Privacy law

Your site should include a privacy policy that makes it clear what information is collected about visitors and how it will be used. Don't forget to disclose any information that's automatically gathered by your server's traffic reports, especially if this anonymous information can later be linked to a person's identity.

Under laws in the EU and the US, people have a right to decide how personal data about them will be used. Personal data is any information that can identify a living person or enable someone to contact them, but that could be just an e-mail address. That alone can reveal someone's name and employer. Pseudonyms don't absolve sites of responsibility to comply either, since they identify people to others who know them by that name.

Under EU law, you can't export personal data outside the European Economic Area without the consent of the people whose data is being exported. If you have foreign offices you might need to share information with, you'll need to cover this in your privacy policy. If you're using external contractors, you'll need to get written confirmation that they will only use the data according to your instructions and the consent that's been obtained.

If a website is aimed at children, or is a general audience website collecting personal data from children, it might need to comply with the US Children's Online Privacy Protection Act. This imposes an obligation to get parental consent before collecting personal information from children.

Even where there isn't a legal requirement, website visitors expect ethical sites to look after their data and not share it. Websites should conduct any direct marketing on behalf of advertisers themselves, and not just hand over the database.

Make sure that all information you hold on people is well secured and protected from unauthorized access, and tell people how they can have their data deleted from your files.

Promotional laws

Most countries have laws controlling misleading advertising, but what they see as deceptive varies. Comparative advertising is banned in some countries and you have to focus on the strengths of your product and not the weaknesses of a competitor's. Under US law, any claims made in an advert must be supported by evidence and adverts must disclose anything likely to affect the buying decision.

Make sure that your promotional claims are accurate and substantiated with any sources for statistics. This also enhances the credibility of your sales message.

If you're running a prize draw or competition to promote your website, you might fall under gambling legislation. If participants have to give you something valuable to take part (and that might include information) and the prize is based on chance, it could be seen as an illegal lottery under US law. You can limit your exposure by offering a mail-in option to take part in the draw.

If you're engaging in distance selling for the first time, make sure that your terms and conditions cover your trading terms too. Under EU law, customers have a seven-day cooling-off period during which they can cancel an order and the contract terminates if the goods aren't supplied in 30 days unless a later date was agreed when the order was placed. If customers aren't properly notified of the price, terms and conditions and business address, their right to cancel the contract is extended by three months, so make sure all pertinent information is confirmed by e-mail.

Restricting liability through terms and conditions

You must incorporate a limitation of liability into your website's terms and conditions and make them a requirement for using the site. Some lawyers argue that the conditions aren't binding unless the site visitors have to view them before using the site and agree to them, but few websites include such a barrier to entry. When customers are placing an order or contributing content to the site, you can provide a box they have to tick to indicate they've read the terms and conditions. You might have separate terms and conditions for accessing the website and for conducting business with it.

Because websites are internationally available, there's a debate about how far national laws can be applied to them. Clearly websites can't be above the law, but it's extremely difficult and costly to have to comply with every law in every country, especially since many of these conflict with each other. If your activities are banned in a particular country, make it clear that your offer is not open to residents of that country.

The terms and conditions of using the site should also:

- clarify copyright. Make it clear who owns the site and the contents, and who owns the copyright in anything visitors contribute while at the site. Include a copyright notice on the website and make it clear how the material there can be used. Can schools print it and copy it for classes to study? Are users allowed to make only one copy, or are they invited to give a copy to all their friends?

■ disclaim links. Make it clear that you're not responsible for anything found on other websites;

■ limit liability and disclaim warranties. Tell readers they access the site at their own risk, and you're not liable for any damage they incur doing so. This might not be enforceable in all countries;

■ choose the law that will be used to govern any disputes, but be aware that customers might be able to make orders subject to their national law irrespective of this term;

■ establish a venue for disputes. You don't want to fly all over the world defending a court case. Bring any disputes home to you;

■ make it clear how responsibility for security is shared. Make visitors liable for their passwords and user IDs;

■ establish a mechanism for changing these terms. Do you need to tell all the visitors by e-mail, or can you just post an update on the website?

■ disclaim the availability and performance of the website. Don't be held responsible if the server crashes when someone needs to access the site.

Tell site visitors where they can contact you if they want to raise concerns about copyright infringement or libel and have a system in place to respond to inquiries quickly. Swift action in deleting content can prevent courtroom dramas later. You don't want to stifle free speech, but you can exercise the choice over how much risk you carry.

Checklist: website law

Run this quick checklist on your site, but remember that it's no substitute for professional advice.

Technology

■ Have you checked that your domain name, search engine keywords and page titles don't include unauthorized trade marks?

- Have you conducted a patent search?
- Have you tested whether your site is accessible to the disabled?

Content

- Is the content honest and true?
- Can you prove it?
- If not, do you have the permission of any potential libel litigants to publish your claims?
- Do you have the permission of creators to use any content you didn't create?
- Do you have model release forms for photography?
- Have you checked no trade marks are used generically?
- Does your site make clear how you will use site visitors' contributions and seek their consent?
- Have you reached an agreement about how you can use your website design and who owns the copyright?
- Have you rated your content using PICS?

Links

- Have you got the permission of the site you're linking to?
- Have you checked sites you link to for libel?
- Have you included a disclaimer for the content of linked sites?

Privacy law

- Have you told visitors how their data will be used?
- Do you have a written contract with your site host governing how they will process data for you?
- Have you taken steps to protect the data?
- Do you have consent to export data to your foreign offices?
- Do you make children obtain parental consent?
- Do you tell people how they can have their data deleted?

Business

- Have you justified any claims in your advertising?

- Are you giving your visitors the chance to opt out of mailings?

- Do your sales terms and conditions set a jurisdiction for any legal disputes?

- Have you checked for and solved any potential legal conflicts in markets abroad?

- Have you excluded any countries you know have laws against your practices?

- Have you got a mechanism in place for fielding complaints promptly?

Summary

When you set up your website, you become a publisher for the first time and expose yourself to international laws. Some of these will conflict and you'll need to use your terms and conditions to limit your liability.

Other laws follow consistent principles, even if countries interpret cases differently. You'll need to clarify how you can use any content on your site that comes from outside the business and you'll need to vet your content for libel. You'll also need to check that you're not using someone else's brand names or technology without permission.

Check that your links don't create an impression of an alliance between different websites and don't encourage the spread of libel.

There's also a moral responsibility to make your site accessible to the disabled, to rate it for potentially offensive content and to protect personal data that visitors disclose to you.

You can't imagine every interpretation of every law worldwide, so invite visitors to contact you before they contact their lawyers. Respond promptly to any complaints and you can cut the risk of having to go to court.

Measuring your website's success

You wouldn't measure the effectiveness of a shop by how many times the door swings open, yet business that obsess about how many people come into their website do exactly that

Introduction

What if one small change to your website could double the money it makes? Or what if most of your website visitors were leaving at the homepage and not even seeing all the goodies you've prepared deeper in the site?

To answer questions like these, you need to be able to measure your website's success and who's visiting it. But you can't rely on visitor levels to tell the whole story, as this chapter reveals.

This is the last chapter in the book, but it's also the start of the next generation of your website. You can find out what people are seeing (and what they aren't) to help you when deciding what content to create or how to redesign the site. Before planning your next promotional wave, work out what was most effective last time.

You can't manage what you don't measure, so make sure you measure anything that influences your website's success.

Know what to measure

You wouldn't measure the effectiveness of a shop by how many times the door swings open, yet businesses that obsess about how many people come into their website do exactly that.

Visitor levels form part of the success formula, but they're too crude alone to help you improve the site's effectiveness. If your site should sell, the bottom line is how many sales it gets and visitor levels are relevant only if they help you to work out how sales can be increased. Remember why you set up the website (as discussed in Chapter 2) and use this to guide what you measure.

- If your site aims to increase how often customers shop with you, find out how often customers return. Find out which promotions generate the most frequent shoppers.

- If you're trying to make money from carrying adverts, find out how many pages people read and how often they return. Find out which adverts generate most money, and which positions on screen work best.

- If you're trying to build your reputation, find out how many other websites link to yours. Find out how many people are using your referral mechanism to recommend your site to friends. Try to find out how aware your target market is of your company, and what they think your brand represents.

- If you're trying to move business online to cut your costs, work out how many of your walk-in customers have switched to dealing online. Check whether you've lost any customers along the way. Keep strict tabs on what your website is costing so that your costs don't go up.

- If you're trying to extend your global reach through your website, find out which countries your visitors and website customers come from and which foreign search engines you are listed on.

You can learn a lot from the technical reports your site generates, but you'll get buried in irrelevant data if you aren't selective. Pick out the information that really tells you how you're progressing towards your website's goals.

There are two main ways to measure the level of website visitors (also known as the website traffic): using counters and analyzing server logs.

Using counters

Counters are pictures that you embed in your web page. Each time the image is sent out, a running total is increased. The number of times that the graphic is sent by the server should be the same as the number of times the page has been viewed, but it's never totally accurate. Some visitors won't be using graphics and others will move on to a new page before the counter, typically one of the last page elements, downloads. Trends in visitors should be fairly accurate though, because you would expect the number of failed counters to stay about the same to the proportion of visitors over time.

The counter image often shows the running total of visitors, but the image can be anything. It can be a logo or picture, or can even be invisible or so tiny that visitors don't notice it. Whatever it is, it needs to download quickly (see Chapter 5 for tips on making pictures load quickly).

More advanced counters can keep track of what browser, screen size and computer the visitor is using and which page they came from before visiting your site. These counters won't work fully if the visitor has disabled Javascript in their browser or is using a browser that doesn't support it. (Javascript is one way to make web pages interactive.)

Counters are popular because they're widely available for free and they're easy to install. But some of them will force you to show advertising to your visitors, some will delete traffic records after a short while, and some will make your statistics available to everyone. Most of the free counters will require you to link to the site offering the service.

One weakness of counters is that they have to be installed on each page you're interested in and will usually give separate statistics for each page, which you will have to compare yourself. Many website designers will put a counter on the homepage, but that will tell you only how many people found their way to your website. It gives you no measure of what content they were most interested in, or even whether they left straight away expecting to find something else.

There are plenty of counters around, so if you use one choose one that:

- doesn't reveal your traffic information to anyone else. Your competitors could exploit this and customers will lose faith in a website that obviously isn't getting much support because the traffic is low. All websites start with low traffic;
- is discreet and looks good;
- doesn't put advertising on your website.

Some of the free counters will reserve these features for paid upgrades, but the prices are negligible and it's worth the investment. See this book's website (www.sbwtw.com) where you will find links to several counters.

©Nik Scott Illustrations, nikscott.com

Analyzing server logs

A counter is a cheap substitute for server logs, which enable you to track what was really sent out from your website's server. A record can be kept of each file that was sent, together with the time and the computer that requested it.

While counters can only keep track of how many times the counter image downloaded (and then infer how often the page they're on downloaded), server logs will record every text page, file, program and graphic that downloads.

In their raw form, these lists are not much use. But there are commercial packages that will identify trends and plot graphs based on the logs. They'll tell you what time people are visiting, where in the world they come from and which ISP they use. They'll tell you how many pages they read, how long they spend on the site, which link they followed to arrive there, and much more. If you are selling advertising on your website directly, advertisers will want to know this type of information.

There are different ways of measuring the same traffic to a website. Imagine a visitor (let's call her Karen) comes to your site and goes from your homepage to your links page. Each page has five pictures on it. This is how that action might be reflected in your visitor reports.

Example of a Webtrends report

Webtrends reports will turn the server logs into easily-understandable graphs and tables of who is visiting the website, where they come from in the world, how they find the website, what they see on the site and how long they stay there. This is an extract from a sample report that runs to 29 pages. Reports can be configured for the information they deliver. (Sample report courtesy of Webtrends.)

Most Accessed Directories

This section analyzes accesses to the directories of the site. This information can be useful in determining the types of data most often requested.

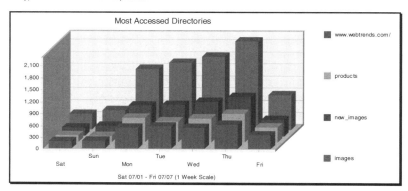

	Path to Directory	Hits	% of Total Hits	Non Cached %	Non Cached K Xferred	Visitor Sessions
1	http://www.webtrends.com/images	119,905	65.19%	66.18%	152,089	9,000
2	http://www.webtrends.com/new_images	19,371	10.53%	67.14%	36,072	4,345
3	http://www.webtrends.com/products	6,649	3.61%	80.31%	51,075	3,247
4	http://www.webtrends.com/	5,916	3.21%	100%	48,820	3,070
5	http://www.webtrends.com/include	2,406	1.3%	54.94%	435	2,140
6	http://www.webtrends.com/awards	3,484	1.89%	89.09%	9,933	2,134
7	http://www.webtrends.com/customers	2,132	1.15%	92.49%	6,567	1,378
8	http://www.webtrends.com/partners	1,729	0.94%	86.92%	4,069	1,224
9	http://www.webtrends.com/redirect	1,141	0.62%	100%	702	1,001
10	http://www.webtrends.com/ads	1,354	0.73%	96.89%	9,706	988
11	http://www.webtrends.com/support	2,261	1.22%	83.28%	23,393	737
12	http://www.webtrends.com/graphics	1,926	1.04%	85.92%	10,463	617
13	http://www.webtrends.com/SampleReports	3,379	1.83%	78.98%	80,882	590
14	http://www.webtrends.com/site_download	928	0.5%	93.96%	14,539	580
15	http://www.webtrends.com/loganalyzer	1,817	0.98%	99.66%	261,554	497
16	http://www.webtrends.com/reports	1,093	0.59%	87.46%	13,713	350
17	http://www.webtrends.com/order	870	0.47%	92.87%	8,000	304
18	http://www.webtrends.com/styles	314	0.17%	83.12%	146	297
19	http://www.webtrends.com/download	1,402	0.76%	99.07%	763,346	294
20	http://www.webtrends.com/cgi-bin	378	0.2%	100%	1,815	223

Most Accessed Directories - Help Card

? This section analyzes accesses to your site's directories. The table lists the most accessed directories in decreasing order of the number of hits. Non-Cached % represents the percentage of hits that were not already in the visitor's browser cache. Use this information to determine the types of data most often requested.
Tip: To focus your report, consider using the Directory filter to include or exclude directories and sub-directories.

♀ These trends indicate the content visitors are most interested in. Use this information to determine content areas to develop, which to focus on less, and how to arrange your content for optimal effect.

Visitors by Number of Visits During Report Period

This section shows the distribution of visitors based on how many times each visitor visited your site.

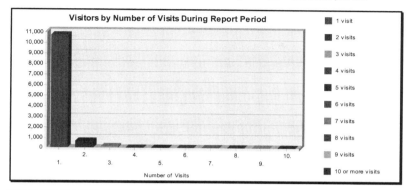

Visitors by Number of Visits During Report Period		
Number of Visits	**Number of Visitors**	**% of Total Unique Visitors**
1 visit	10768	92.11%
2 visits	699	5.97%
3 visits	140	1.19%
4 visits	38	0.32%
5 visits	17	0.14%
6 visits	5	0.04%
7 visits	4	0.03%
8 visits	2	0.01%
9 visits	3	0.02%
10 or more visits	14	0.11%

Visitors by Number of Visits During Report Period - Help Card

? This section shows the distribution of visitors based on how many times each visitor visited your site. This covers visits made during the reporting period only; a visitor's visits before or after the reporting period do not contribute to the visitor's visit count.

♀ This statistic is an indication of whether or not your site compels return visits. Updating web site content is one way to improve this statistic.

Continued

Example of a Webtrends report (continued)

New vs. Returning Visitors

This section shows the number of first-time visitors to your site and the number of returning visitors to your site. Only visitors identified by cookies are counted. First-time visitors are those who didn't have a cookie on their 1st hit, but had one on later hits. Returning visitors are those who already had a cookie on their 1st hit (their previous visit happened before the start of this report period.)

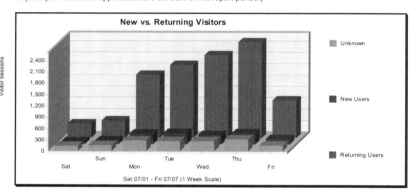

New vs. Returning Visitors		
New or Returning Visitor	**Number of Visitor Sessions**	**% of Total Sessions**
Returning Users	10,235	76.86%
New Users	1,481	11.12%
Unknown	1,601	12.02%

New vs. Returning Visitors - Help Card

? This section shows the number of first-time visitors to your site and the number of returning visitors to your site. Only visitors who can be identified with cookies are counted. First-time visitors are those who didn't have a cookie on their 1st hits, but had one on later hits. Returning visitors are those who already had a cookie on their 1st hit, and whose previous visit happened before the start of this report period. To get the most accurate information, make sure you set up the Cookies tab in the Options window to properly interpret the cookies you give to visitors.

♀ By considering the ratio between new and returning visitors over a period of time, you can determine if your site is adequately attracting repeat visits. If you consistently have a high number of returning visitors, congratulations; you're doing a good job! However, if you are accustomed to seeing a low number of returning visitors, it's time to figure out why.

Activity Level by Day of the Week

This section shows the activity for each day of the week for the report period (i.e. if there are two Mondays in the report period, the value presented is the sum of all hits for both Mondays.) Values in the table do not include erred hits.

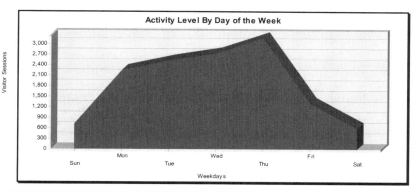

	Day	Hits	% of Total Hits	Visitor Sessions
1	Sun	14,833	8.06%	727
2	Mon	32,944	17.91%	2,248
3	Tue	32,754	17.8%	2,521
4	Wed	33,578	18.25%	2,731
5	Thu	38,039	20.68%	3,175
6	Fri	18,652	10.14%	1,317
7	Sat	13,117	7.13%	598
Total Weekdays		**155,967**	**84.8%**	**11,992**
Total Weekend		**27,950**	**15.19%**	**1,325**

Activity Level by Day of the Week - Help Card

? This section shows the activity for each day of the week for the report period (i.e. if there are two Mondays in the report period, the value presented is the sum of all hits for both Mondays.) The table lists the number of hits, percentage of total hits and visitor sessions for each day of the week for the report period. Values in this table do not include erred hits.

Tip: Consider the Day of Week Filter to include or exclude activity based on the day of the week.

? Days of less activity should be considered for maintenance and content improvement.

Hits

Your hits show the number of files downloaded from the server and each different picture seen is a new hit. Karen registers 12 hits (two pages, plus ten picture files). Hits are not a good measure of success because they're influenced by the design as well as the traffic. A bloated, graphic-heavy website design will score more hits per visitor than a site that is quicker to download and easier to use.

Page views

This tells you how many scrolling pages are downloaded and is a better measure of what people are looking at. Karen's visit represents two page views. If you want to increase your advert exposures, you'll need to increase your page views. You can track how many pages are viewed by each visitor and it's usually easier to double the number of pages seen by visitors already at the site than it is to double the traffic coming to the site.

Visitor sessions

Karen's activities on the site represent one visitor session. If she returned later that day, it would register another session, but she can look at as many pages as she wants all over the site in a single session.

Visitor session length

This tells you how long visitors stay on the site on average. In our example, Karen might have been on the site for half a minute. It's an indication of how much attention visitors are giving your content.

Unique visitors

Karen would be just one unique visitor, even if she returned daily. This will tell you how many different people you have coming to the site, and advertisers are often interested in this because it tells them how many different people their message will reach. The reports will often give these figures by date, as a total for the period the report covers and as an average for each day.

The reports can also show where visitors start and finish on the site and which pages were most and least popular.

One of the most important pages in the report is the top exit page, which tells you where most visitors leave the site. If you're trying to sell from the website, that's where the sales pitch collapses. If that page is your shopping cart, you know they're interested in buying but not prepared to complete payment. Reassure them about security or reconsider how easy it is to use your shopping cart.

If the paths visitors take through your site seem more like bypasses for an important product section, you could run a promotion for that section or give it a more prominent mention on the most popular page on your site.

Your server report will tell you the keywords that visitors used on search engines to reach your site. It will give you a clue about what they're looking for, which keyword phrases you should use more in the site and (by their absence) which search engines you need to improve your listing in. More importantly, it will give you some idea of the relevance of visitors who are coming to your site from search engines.

Technology tips: checking website performance

Not everything you need to know will be shown in your traffic reports or counter totals. Here are some other website success factors you can measure for your website.

- You can find out how many websites are linking to you, and where they are, by using the www.altavista.com search engine. Search for your website address with 'link:' in front of it (e.g. link:www.sbwtw.com).

- Monitor your website availability. You can get software that will try to visit your website regularly to check that it's online and the server hasn't crashed. One such service is at www.netwhistle.com.

- Check your website's download time. You can use www.netmechanic.com to estimate the download time for your page using different connections. If you're going to visit the site yourself to test it, try it at peak time. You can find out when that is from your server reports.

- You can use software tools that check your ranking in search engines against specific keywords. The success of this depends on you correctly second-guessing the keywords that visitors will want to use to find your type of website. See Chapter 9 for more on how search engines work so that you can improve your ranking.

- If you want to test the effectiveness of various promotional methods, make different entry pages to the website which greet visitors with appropriate offers depending on where they've come from. In the reports (or by using counters), you'll be able to rank the pages in order of popularity to tell which promotion worked best.

- If advertising is important to your business plan and you're being paid for each clickthrough, set up a mechanism for checking how often adverts are clicked. Once you've developed it, you can also use it to keep tabs on how visitors use the site's navigation.

Measuring in your business

You can't measure all success factors automatically. You'll need to introduce systems in your business to track the website's impact on it. Here are a few ideas.

- Ask your shop and phone customers where they heard about you, so you can tell how many read the website and were encouraged by it to make contact.

- Keep track of the type and value of sales the website generates.

- Keep track of the types of customers the website attracts. Does it bring in a few big spenders or lots of infrequent buyers?

- Ask customers in the shop whether they've been to your website and how it might be improved.

Carrying out surveys

If you need to find out more about your customers, why don't you ask them? The web is the ideal medium for gathering information if you structure your survey well. But be prepared to offer your visitors something for their participation: an entry in a competition or access to hidden website content can be cheap incentives.

Your survey will be easiest to analyze and will be easier to complete if you include closed questions where visitors select one of several options or tick multiple boxes. Try to vary the question format and minimize the number of questions. You should also invite comments and suggest that visitors send any other feedback by e-mail, so that your survey design doesn't stop visitors from telling you what they feel most strongly about, even if you didn't think to survey it.

When posing questions, try to be specific so that they aren't open to diverse interpretations. If you ask visitors whether they visit your site often, you won't learn anything because it depends on what they consider to be often. It means something totally different to say you read a newspaper often and you holiday in France often. Be specific and ask whether they visit your website daily, weekly or monthly on average. You should determine this frequency by how often you update content and how visitors use your site.

Don't ask questions that are too taxing. Questions that ask visitors to rank lists in order of importance are difficult to finish once the customer has eliminated their clear preferences. Give them a neutral position as well, so that they're not forced to say whether they like or dislike something. That will skew results from those who really are impartial. You can't expect visitors to care as deeply about your website as you do.

Ideally, you'd like an e-mail address for each participant and would like them to sign up for a newsletter from your site. But don't force them to give their details if they don't want to. You can analyze data from named customers and anonymous ones separately, but you might discover the most valuable comments come from those who want to confide in secret.

Remember that your survey results reflect only the opinions of those who participated. You can't generalize the results to say they represent your whole customer base, or even all your website visitors. Those most willing to help you are often the ones who have used similar surveys before and have greater experience with the Internet. If you're going to ask questions that will be affected by online experience (such as how easy your site is to use), ask customers how long they've been using the web. Try to account for anything that's obviously going to skew the results.

Making the stats work for you

Once you start combining the different stats in your server reports and linking them to your business information, you can learn about the quality of visitors and not just their quantity.

Knowing you've got 500 page views won't tell you how to increase them unless you also know how many real people are visiting. If you've got one person looking at 500 pages, there's an opportunity to bring more people into the site. But if you have 500 people looking at one page each, your best chance for growth is to encourage each visitor to view more pages while they're on the site.

In a similar way, you need to keep track of the orders that come in. There's no point knowing that your total revenue is high if you can't tell whether that's because you have a few high-value customers or lots of low-value shoppers.

You might know that half your visitors come back every day, but what if most regular readers are interested in only one section of your site? Instead of thinking that half your visitors really like your site, you know that half your customers for particular products come back daily and the rest aren't that fussed. And are these customers buying as much as you'd like them to? Knowing this, you can make plans.

The trick to making your visitor information work for you is not to focus on interpreting what you're given. Instead tell your technical team what you need to know about customers and how they use your site to be able to judge the website's success.

Summary

Decide how you can measure your progress towards your site's goal and analyze the information that affects that. Don't get hung up on increasing hits, for example, if your goal is to increase sales. Use your visitor information instead to find ways of improving sales, such as increasing the number of customers you have or the amount they spend.

You can use counters or server reports to analyze your website traffic. Reports will tell you much more than counters and will be invisible to visitors, but you'll have to pay for them.

Not all the information you need will be available in those reports. Some of it will need the technical team to set up other measurement tools, but you'll need systems in the business to trap important data there too. If you need to learn more about customers, set up a survey on your website.

Websites can be improved and refined continuously, becoming more and more effective at growing your company with each upgrade. The changes need not be expensive or daring – a new navbar might make the site easier to use, or a brief explanation might increase confidence in your sales and bump up incoming orders. When you re-promote your site, create new content for it, introduce new product lines or revamp the design, check first how the site is performing now to make sure that you don't repeat any mistakes or false assumptions.

With careful planning, testing what works and aggressive promotion, you'll see that you can have a website for your small business that really does work.

11 Measuring your website's success

Glossary

Affiliate programme

A scheme where you are paid for referring customers to another website by including a link to it on your website.

Attachment

A file (such as a word-processing document, a spreadsheet or a picture file) that is sent with an e-mail message. Recipients will need to use a program like the one that created the file to read it, even if they can understand the e-mail message it accompanied without needing any extra programs.

Autoresponder

A program that issues an immediate standardized response to incoming e-mail.

Bookmark

A shortcut to a web page. When you bookmark a web page, the browser stores its title and address. Next time you want to visit that page, you just need to select it from the bookmarks list. In Internet Explorer, bookmarks are called favourites. You can have as many bookmarks as you want.

Browser

A program used to read web pages. Leading browsers include Microsoft Internet Explorer, Netscape Navigator and Opera.

Content

The words, pictures, videos, sounds and programs that you put on your website.

Database

A collection of organized, searchable information.

Directory

A hierarchically structured guide to websites.

Domain name

The part of the website address that is common to the addresses of all the pages on the website. In the address www.sbwtw.com/index.htm the domain name is www.sbwtw.com. The domain name identifies the server where the website is stored.

Download

To copy files (including web pages) over an Internet connection into your computer.

E-commerce

Electronic commerce usually refers to trading conducted over the Internet.

E-mail

Short for electronic mail. Computer messages that are addressed to individual people and stored in a mailbox. People connect to the Internet and use e-mail software to download their messages. Appropriate software includes Outlook and Eudora. There are also websites, such as www.hotmail.com, that will let you access your e-mail using a web browser. An e-mail address always has an @ sign in it, and often follows the format name@domainname.com.

Favourites

See Bookmark.

Filter

Incoming e-mail can be sorted automatically using filters which direct the e-mail to appropriate folders. Someone might have e-mail from their friends go into a folder called 'friends' and have junk mail automatically sent to the Trash folder unread. Filtering software can also be used to block access to certain websites based on words they contain, for example to protect children from sites that include swearing.

Firewall

A program that polices all the communications going between a computer and the Internet. If unauthorised programs try to hack in, or viruses try to send out messages, the firewall will block them.

Forms

Forms enable data to be entered into web pages for processing by the server. They can include text boxes of different sizes, round buttons of which only one can be selected (e.g. 'yes or no'), square checkboxes of which any number can be selected (e.g. 'I like chocolate, tea and toast') and buttons which tell the browser to process the information when clicked.

Graphics

Pictures on a computer screen.

Hoax virus warning

Chain letters that spread fear and alarm about viruses that don't exist.

Homepage

The first page that you see when you type in the website address. The browser's homepage is the page that opens up whenever the browser is started, or when the 'Home' button on the browser is clicked.

Host

A server.

Icon

On a web page, an icon is a small picture that shows what the associated link does. An icon of an envelope might represent an e-mail link. Outside of web pages, icons are often used to represent different files so they can be moved around the hard disk with the mouse and can be opened by clicking on them.

Internet

A global network of computers that enables data and e-mail messages to be distributed quickly worldwide. The world wide web and newsgroups are built on top of the Internet technology.

ISP (Internet service provider)

A company that provides a user's connection to the Internet, often using a phone line, cable modem or dedicated high-speed line.

Keyword

A word used when searching for information on a computer to tell the computer what you're looking for.

Link

Text or a picture on a web page which when clicked will take you to a different page. Links can be formed between any two files anywhere on the Internet and can jump to the middle of a file as well. Links are one-way, but the back button on the browser can be used to return. Reciprocal links are where two sites agree to link to each other.

Log

A record of all the files sent out from a website's server.

Navbar

Short for 'navigation bar', this is a panel with links to other parts of the same website. It's often made of graphics that look like buttons.

Navigation

Used to refer to how people find their way around websites.

Newsgroup

A discussion group that uses the Internet but is independent of the world wide web. Newsreader software is used to access newsgroups. Some websites allow people to read and post messages to newsgroups but are only providing a gateway to the newsgroups: they don't own them and the newsgroups can still be reached without going through that website.

Pixels

The dots that make up a screen display.

Plug-in

Programs that enable browsers to process web pages containing new types of file from the Internet, such as virtual reality models, interactive animations or music.

Pop-up

A window that opens up on top of the existing window and is usually smaller than the main window.

Portal

A website that provides a start page for people coming on to the Internet. Typical portals offer a search engine, the latest news headlines, shopping facilities and free web e-mail accounts.

Resolution

This refers to the amount of detail a user can see on their computer screen and is unrelated to the screen's physical size. A typical resolution for a PC is 800 pixels wide by 600 pixels deep.

Scroll

In olden times, paper scrolls would be unfurled at the bottom and rolled up at the top to see a new page. Scrolling the screen is similar: the document is moved up or down through the window, or left or right, so that a different part of it can be seen.

Search engine

A website that has a vast database of web pages all over the Internet that you can search by keyword to find what you need.

Server

The computer that stores your website and makes it available to the Internet, sending out the web pages as they are requested by website visitors.

Shareware

Software that is free for anybody to copy and try out, but which must be registered and paid for if it's used beyond the trial period.

Shopping cart

A page on a website where you can store items you're interested in buying before confirming the sale. It enables shoppers to buy multiple items in one transaction.

Signature

A few lines of text that are automatically added to the end of an e-mail by your e-mail program. These are used to include contact details and disclaimers, but can include any message.

Sitemap

A directory of one website with links to all of the pages on it.

Spam

Junk e-mail.

Surfing the web

Spending time visiting websites and following links between them, exploring where they lead.

Traffic

The number of visitors a website gets.

URL

Short for universal resource locator. Each web page has its own URL, which uniquely identifies that page on the web. The URL is shown in the browser's location box and by typing it in you can go straight to a particular web page.

Virus

A hidden program capable of copying itself between disks and computers, and often able to spread itself by stowing away on e-mails. These programs can cause considerable damage by deleting files on machines they infect.

Web page

A document that's viewed over the worldwide web that can include text, graphics, animation, forms and interactive features. Pages that don't fit on a single screen can be scrolled in the browser window.

Website

A group of web pages that are operated by the same person and usually have a common theme and the same domain name.

Website address

To get to a website, you type in its website address. For websites that have bought their own domain name, the website address is the same as the domain name. Others might have a website address that is based on their hosting company's domain name.

Window

A box on screen in which a program runs, or information is shown.

World wide web

The web sits on top of the Internet and makes it easier to exchange information. The web has popularized the Internet and made it easy to create and publish web pages, and to find and read them.

Index